Natalie

See you at

The TOP!

[signature]

7-9-16

ID963033

johnharemza@aol.com

"An excellent read. Sage advice on Network Marketing by an industry Legend."

–Jordan Adler, International Bestselling Author of *Beach Money* and Global Philanthropist

"John's not 'almost right' about network marketing success. He's spot-on with what it takes to be successful in network marketing — and in life. Listen to this man. Follow his advice. And you might be surprised how successful you become."

–Dan Waldschmidt, Award Winning Author of *Edgy Conversations* and Elite Ultrarunner

"John is a legend in Direct Sales. His $15 million in career earnings speaks for itself. Right or Almost Right is an absolute must read for anyone in the profession."

–Ken Dunn, Million Dollar MLM Earner and Author of *The Greatest Prospector In The World*

"John Haremza is one of the most resilient people I know. I've watched him overcome obstacles and setbacks that would overwhelm most people. He does it with rare blend of courage, determination and a commitment to keeping things simple. John started with very little of what the world thinks is necessary for success. He heard all the reasons why he couldn't succeed by all the people who knew him. Fortunately he trusted himself and he treasured his dreams. His story is one that will inspire you to do the same."

–Stewart Hughes, CEO and Chairman of the Board, Unicity International

"What John has described in this book is EXACTLY the difference between those who achieve great results from those who have average results. The best of the best are those who strive for excellence at the 'right' things. When you implement what you learn in this book, your personal results will improve, and you will become a better coach and leader of your organization."

–**Todd Smith**, $27 Million Career Earner and Author of
Little Things Matter

"Love, love, love your book. We always knew you were amazing! Thanks for sharing with us"!

–**Steve and Melyn Campbell**, Co-Founders of
Limitless Worldwide

"Right or Almost Right is a must read for every networker. Good intentions and working hard give some networkers the feeling that they're on the right track, yet they become disappointed when things just don't seem to work out. When they make the slight modifications that John masterfully teaches, things seem to come together seamlessly—they become Right, not Almost Right—and success follows."

–**Nate Cox**, Top Executive at Sound Concepts

"Success leaves clues! In his book, Right or Almost Right *John Haremza guides you through the obstacles and challenges you will face as a home based entrepreneur. A must read for anyone looking to succeed in Network Marketing."*

–**David Skultety**, Lifestyle Entrepreneur and 7-Figure Earner

RIGHT OR
ALMOST RIGHT

JOHN HAREMZA

RIGHT OR ALMOST RIGHT

The Fine Line Between Phenomenal Success and Average Results in Network Marketing

Right or Almost All Right
The Fine Line Between Phenomenal Success and Average Results in Network Marketing

Copyright ©2015 by John Haremza
All rights reserved.

Published by Next Century Publishing
Las Vegas, Nevada
www.NextCenturyPublishing.com

No part of this publication may be reproduced, stored in a retrieval system, or transmitted in any form or by any means—electronic, mechanical, photocopy, recording, or any other—without the prior permission of the author.

ISBN: 978-1-68102-052-5
Library of Congress Control Number: 2015944351

Printed in the United States of America

I'm particularly grateful for my parents, family and friends who have been so supportive.

I'd like to thank my many mentors and those who have influenced my life over the past 25 years including Jim Rohn, Jeff Roberti, Eric Worre, Todd Smith, and Randy Schroeder. I especially appreciate so many individuals I have worked with over the years.

I appreciate the assistance from:

Illustrations and charts designed by Kelli Jo Steiner

Editing by Lisa Kass and Becky Morris

Special thanks to my long-time assistant, Peter Lees, who made this book possible.

And last I have to thank all those dream stealers who said I could not do it. They gave me an unshakable determination to succeed.

My wish for you is that you will see your dreams
become your reality.

If I can live the life of my dreams with my background,

then you can live the life of your dreams with your background.

FOREWORD

We will all encounter seemingly insurmountable challenges over the course of our lifetimes. That is a reality that we cannot escape. However, when these situations arise, we must ask ourselves: "How am I going to face these hardships? What will I learn from them? How will I change and grow? Will I become bitter, or better?" My friend, John Haremza, has faced many challenges his entire life. And he's had to answer these same questions.

After being labeled as "slow" and "stupid", and bullied from a young age, John was eventually diagnosed as dyslexic and told, "You'll never amount to nothing." So how did this nothing-of-a-man go on to earn over $14 million, enabling him to travel the globe and own a million-dollar lakeside home? He discovered the difference between doing things right, and doing them almost right. He learned to make small decisions—such as not allowing others to determine who he was or what his destiny would be—and he chose to make important daily changes that have led him to the success he now enjoys. John calls this his "Small-Step Philosophy." One of his beliefs is that it is far less damaging to try something and risk failure, than it is to live with the resentment of never having tried at all. This mindset has led him to the definitive conclusion that the rewards of network marketing far outweigh any risk of failure.

As a network marketer, I'm sure you've been told, "This will never work; your plan will never work." You now have a choice: will you listen to those naysayers, or will you continue to work your plan and learn how to do things right, instead of almost right, from people like John? Throughout the book you are about to read, you'll find many examples of John's Small-Step Philosophy. On every page you'll see the value of applying his ways of thinking to your life, to your business, and to your relationships. In fact, if you make a decision to implement the principles in this book, in your later years you'll be able to look back on your life with contentment and satisfaction.

I encourage you to read this book not just once, but several times. You'll discover how John learned the network marketing business from the ground, up—just like you are doing. But the best part is that you'll learn both what worked and what didn't work for him, so that you can follow his path to success! Then you'll be able to do for others what John is doing for you. You can show them the difference between doing things *Right or Almost Right!*

Your friend and fellow network marketer,

Jordan Adler
Author, Beach Money
Network Marketing Millionaire

TABLE OF CONTENTS

RIGHT OR
ALMOST RIGHT

The question is,
"Are you doing it right or almost right?"

INTRODUCTION

Thank you for your decision to purchase this book. I have structured it as a conversation between a new distributor and myself to answer the questions that someone new to network marketing typically asks. Questions such as:

- ✓ What am I doing right or almost right?
- ✓ How should I approach a prospect?
- ✓ How can I build my business?

Right or almost right: what does this mean?

I've been in the network marketing industry for twenty-five years now. In that time, I've earned just over 14 million dollars. I've travelled the world, learned so many lessons, and witnessed some remarkable success stories.

BUT...

I've also met many incredibly sharp and hard-working individuals who seem to be doing everything right, but they're still not experiencing the success for which they'd hoped. In fact, many of them are struggling.

The question is, "Why?" Are they building their network marketing business right or almost right?

Throughout this book, I give many examples of the subtle differences between right and almost right activities. These small nuances are the difference between struggling and thriving, making a little money or a lot of money, and experiencing frustration or celebration.

In this book you will find examples of my personal philosophy, "Small Steps to the Top," and the impact it has had on my life, as well as the impact I know it can have on yours.

Simply stated, every decision you make, regardless of how small or insignificant it seems at the time, has an impact on your success in life. Where you are today, in every aspect of your life, is a direct result of decisions you've made along the way.

I promise that if you understand and embrace the impact of my "Small Step Philosophy," it will change your life.

It was all small steps.

There were no giant quantum leaps,

just small steps.

I never did anything great,

just small steps.

I never took any great risks,

just small steps.

I took small steps,

everyday, everyday, everyday.

CHAPTER 1

IT WAS ALL SMALL STEPS

*Network marketing can change your life
in ways beyond your imagination.*

John, how did you go from being a dyslexic maintenance manager to being a millionaire? Where did it all start? What got you there? What steps did you take?

My "Small Step" philosophy came into being one quiet summer evening as I sat on my dock watching a beautiful sunset. The questions just popped into my mind: How did all of this happen? How did I get here? How did a dyslexic maintenance manager, written off by everyone as slow and stupid, get to own three homes, travel the globe, have friends around the world, speak to thousands, and live a life I could not have imagined?

Almost every day I drive by the trailer park where I once lived in a 12x70-foot 1969 Garland trailer. Now, here I am, watching the sunset from the dock of my million-dollar lake home, surrounded by all of my toys. What happened to change my life so dramatically?

There was one simple answer. It all came from small steps. I made no quantum leaps, never did anything spectacular, and I didn't take any incredible risks. I just took small steps.

I took small steps every day, every day, every day.

In fact, I am the master of the small step. This is a wonderful affirmation. Why? It is because greatness is in the moment. Greatness is in the moment of decision. The small steps you must take to the top of the mountain are easy steps. Success is made up of thousands of small, seemingly insignificant steps.

What are the small steps that will take you to the top of your mountain? And what are the subtleties of taking those small steps right or almost right that will keep you moving toward success? Let's find out.

The Small Step Philosophy

Every step counts.
Every step is easy to take.
Every step is easy not to take.
Every step is a step up, or a step down.
Every day, every day, every day, every step counts.
Every step takes you closer to, or further from your "WHY."

When you take small steps to the top, every day, every day, every day, the day will come when you will look around in amazement at what you have accomplished.

CHAPTER 2

THE DREAM BEGINS

How did all of this happen? How did I get here?

John, how did you first hear about network marketing? Who introduced you to the concept?

I remember the day I learned about network marketing as if it were yesterday. Dan Sweere, a good friend, invited me to his house on a Wednesday evening so I could take a look at a new water filter business he was considering. Being a maintenance manager, I assumed that he wanted me to check the product to determine if it was well built, give him some advice on the product, and possibly build a display for it—something of that nature.

We'd had a serious problem at the plant where I worked, so I didn't get to Dan's house until after 9:00 p.m. I walked in two hours late in my blue work clothes, covered with grease from head to toe. We wore hairnets because of the food environment in which we worked, and I still had my hairnet on, along with my protective glasses. As it turned out, I hadn't been invited because of my maintenance background. Dan wanted to introduce me to the business opportunity too.

Going to this meeting was an example of a small-step decision. I kept my word that I would be there, even after an exhausting twelve-hour day. All I really wanted to do was to go home and collapse on the couch.

"We Just Waited Two Hours for This Guy?"

When I arrived, I was introduced to two guys in suits. They drove down from Minneapolis to present the business to Dan, three of our buddies, and me. I referred to them as "suits" because back then I didn't own one. I could almost hear them thinking, "We just waited two hours to talk to this guy?" They must have been internally shaking their heads in disbelief at what they saw. They had come 200 miles to this town in the middle of nowhere, in the cold of winter, to meet with a maintenance manager!

The first thing the men did was a test. Dan lived on a lake in the country and the water was rusty brown. They hooked up a filter and ran the water through it. The water went from looking and tasting terrible, to being crystal clear and tasting wonderful. My immediate response was, "I need one of these. Everyone needs one of these."

These guys were good. They could tell the story. I got excited. As a matter of fact, we were all excited. I bought four water filters right on the spot. I wrote out a check for $480 and told them not to cash it until Friday when I got paid.

You Never Know Who May Be in the Room!

You never know who's in the room or who might transform your business. Out of the five individuals there, (Dan had invited twelve, but seven didn't show), I was the least likely candidate.

I know that those two suits from Minneapolis were sure that this trip to nowhere in rural Minnesota in the middle of winter was a complete waste of time. I'm sure they contemplated not waiting for this very late maintenance manager.

I was the only one there who bought into the business, and I did it big time. I made a decision to be at the top of the plan. My life has never been the same since that night.

All of this happened in November 1988, and we were getting married in December. I got home at midnight and showed my fiancée, Jana, the load of water filters I had just bought. Needless to say, she was upset. Our wedding was only a month away, and money was tight. Her first question was, "How much did they cost?"

I told her, "Four hundred and eighty dollars, but don't worry. They're going to hold the check till the end of the week." We were in debt, and there I was spending money we didn't have.

Jana was clearly distraught! I said, "Honey, wait 'til you see what this thing does." I hooked up the water filter to the faucet and ran the water, but it didn't change a thing. The water looked and tasted just like it always had. Now, the water we had in town was actually fairly good water. It wasn't chlorinated and it tasted fine, so the filter didn't seem to change the water at all.

Jana's response was, "You need to stop payment on that check right now."

I was still excited, so I went on to tell her that to get involved in the water filter business required only $5,000, and that I was going to invest the money to do it. Now she was convinced that I'd gone off the deep end. Her only relief was thinking that I could never come up with the money to actually do it.

The Trailer Park

At that time, we were living in a 12x70-foot 1969 Garland trailer home with 2x2 walls. These trailers used newspaper for insulation. The frost would spread two feet up the interior walls when it was cold. You could scrape frost off the walls and put it in a drink as ice—that's the type of frost I'm talking about.

We had a natural gas furnace, but something was wrong with it. We didn't have the money to get it repaired. A few times a week, the pilot would blow out. The unit would backfire and blow the cover off the furnace and into the wall. I'd have to go home from work to re-light the furnace. It was an interesting life to say the least. Then, I roll in at midnight, and announce that I was going to invest five thousand dollars in water filters—into some kind of "scam," as Jana believed it to be. No wonder she was skeptical! Five thousand dollars was more than my old trailer was worth.

Everyone Thought I Had Lost It!

Jana talked to my parents, her parents, her brother-in-law, anyone and everyone, trying to get them to convince me that I'd lost my mind. I know she did it with the best of intentions, and with real concern for our welfare. By then everyone could see that I was committed, and my soon-to-be father-in-law thought I was going to put us in the poor house for sure. Finally, as a last resort, Jana said, "I'm not going to marry you if you do this."

I answered, "Do what you've got to do, but I'm going to do this."

I couldn't articulate it at the time, but I believe it to be far less damaging to a relationship to try something and risk failure, than it would be to live with the resentment of never having tried at all. If I had seen others succeed at network marketing and never tried it myself, I never would've been able to forgive Jana or myself. A negative spouse can be a major hurdle in network marketing. Never the less, about six months later, it would be my wife, Jana, who encouraged me to go full-time into the NSA water filter business.

When Jana saw that I was still determined to give it a shot, she said, "Okay, fine. Do it, but let's get our bills paid off first."

My response was, "Honey, at the rate we're going, that's going to take fifteen to twenty years, provided we don't incur any more debt. I'm looking to do this to make money, not spend money."

> *With the best of intentions people will*
> *try to steer you off course, to nudge you*
> *off course, to persuade you off course,*
> *to distract you off course. They will try*
> *to convince you that you are dreaming.*

So, right before our wedding, I went ahead and did it. I got my dad to, reluctantly, co-sign a note for me, and I bought 40 water filters.

The story gets better still...

The water filters showed up the same week we got married. This did not sit well, and tensions ran high. I had taken a week off work, a week most couples would have used to take a honeymoon, but we didn't have the money for that. I used that week to go out to sell water filters.

We were married on December 17th, so this was on December 20th, just days before Christmas. I had no understanding of network marketing at the time, so I started going from house to house, knocking on doors. My hometown of Perham had good water, so I drove to another town forty-five minutes away. Here was this kid knocking on doors, wearing nothing but slacks and a shirt—probably jeans and a shirt, because I don't think I owned slacks back then—with a tie that reached only halfway to his belt and no coat. I think people let me in merely out of kindness, courtesy or pity.

> *I believe that it is far better to try something and*
> *risk failure, than it is to live with the resentment*
> *of never having tried at all.*

Not only that, I was scared. The first time I went to the town, I drove around for two hours trying to decide what to do and get up my nerve. If there were two cars in the driveway, I assumed they had company, so I wouldn't call on them. If there was one car in the driveway, I would think, well, they're probably both not home and I wanted them both to be there, so I wouldn't call on them. I made up every excuse possible not to knock on doors, but I finally did it. I had to do it. I couldn't go home with all those filters. I had no one backing me. What I did have was a lot of pressure on me with everyone saying my plan wasn't going to work.

> *Courage is resistance to fear, mastery of fear.*
> *It is not the absence of fear.*
> **–Mark Twain**

Sometimes I think I should go back and thank everyone who told me that I couldn't do it. That gave me the greatest determination to make it happen. I had burned the bridges behind me, and that gave me the courage to knock on all those doors.

After giving my sales pitch, I used the "puppy dog close." If I could get people to try a filter, they would see the difference in their water, and they would want to keep it. That first day, I got three people to try out a filter.

> *Courage conquers fear.*

Don't Tell a Soul. Promise Me?

My brother was curious about the business, so I took him with me the following week. We went back to the three homes where I had placed a water filter, and I sold one of them. I made $59 on the spot. I bought it for $120 and sold it for $179, wow!

My brother was amazed. "How could you make $59 so fast?" he asked. We thought we were on our way to becoming rich!

My brother wanted in on the business, too.

He was family, so I told him, "Okay, but we have to make a pact that we won't tell a soul about this." Back then I thought, *why would I want to create competition for myself?*

Now, my parents were really upset because I'd dragged my brother into it, and he bought $5,000 worth of filters also. He and I went out two or three times a week. We'd drive to Fergus Falls after work. He took one side of the street while I took the other. We knocked on doors and placed water filters. We probably knocked on 200 doors, and for the most part everyone was nice and tried them, but very few people bought them.

With this experience behind you, what made you decide to go into network marketing full time? You were doing okay as a maintenance manager. Your supervisors appreciated you and your contributions. You had a job for life, your dream job. Why would you leave all of that?

That last question is what my family asked me many times over. "Why would you leave a good, secure job where you are so well respected?"

Ultimately, it was one guy who helped me make that decision. Someone convinced me to go to a meeting, the first network marketing meeting I had ever attended. I'll never forget this man walking across the stage wearing a baseball hat that was dented at the front and bib overalls with one pant leg tucked into his boot and the other pant leg hanging out. Just to complete the picture, he had manure on his boots. Looking back, I think he was missing some teeth. He got up on stage and said he made $10,000 just the past month.

All I Remembered Was $10,000.

I don't know what else was mentioned at the meeting, but I do remember that $10,000. That was when I said, "I can do this," and my enthusiasm soared. I've heard it said that if you set yourself on fire, people will travel for miles to watch you burn. That was exactly what was happening to me. I was on fire! I saw a way out and I was eager. People didn't know what I was talking about, but they wanted to join me because of my enthusiasm.

Their response was, "I don't know what you're doing, but I want to do it, too."

Going door to door is a tough way to get started in network marketing. What got you on the right track?

After I signed up for the water filter business, I never heard from my sponsor again. I'm sure he thought I was just another statistic. One day I called him out of frustration and he told me that Mike Nelson, a leader in NSA, was holding a meeting in Fargo, about 60 miles from my hometown. A friend, my brother and I went to the meeting. We were going to listen to this guy, get motivated and go knocking on doors again. Mike told us how we needed to recruit and sponsor other people instead.

Why Would I Create Competition?

I thought, *why in the world would I want to create my own competition?* All I could see was selling water filters. I couldn't visualize the leverage aspect of network marketing. Mike Nelson was very motivating, so I talked to him after the meeting. I told him how much I'd enjoyed his speech and that we were heading out to knock on some doors.

Mike said, "You know, I made $205,000 last year, and if you'd told me I had to knock on doors, I wouldn't have done it." He then asked who my sponsor was. When I told him, he replied,

"You're in my down line. Come up to my room after the next session."

Mike made $205,000 and he never knocked on a door!

Later on we went up to Mike's room. He explained the recruiting aspects of the business. From that moment on, I had a paradigm shift in the way I did business. I began to recruit. Now I could see that customers got much more excited about making money than they did about spending it. When I talked about selling them a water filter, they had to spend money. But when I talked to them about cashing in on this major industry of water filtration and the direction it was headed, they could see the opportunity. Instead of buying one filter for their own use, they would buy forty of them to start a business. It made a huge difference and I began to make some money.

Even My Family Saw a Difference.

Now, although they were still upset, my family began to see a change in my attitude. I had so much energy that I barely slept. I worked from bell to bell. I would go to work at my maintenance job. The whole time I was there, my head would be spinning as I thought about the business.

One day a week, I would take off early around 3:00 or 4:00 p.m., load up my car with prospective recruits and head for the business briefing three hours away in Minneapolis. We would go to the meeting, get charged up, be home at 1:00 a.m., and head back to work the next morning. Every week I'd take new people to the meeting. People were feeding off my energy. I began to realize that there was a future in what I was doing. I could see it clearly. What's more, my wife Jana began to see it too, and she encouraged me to go full time with it.

Going Full Time

It was when I made the decision to go full time with my business that I got the real heat from my friends, family and co-workers. The teasing and taunting started in earnest. To this day, I can still remember sitting in the break room with some of my co-workers. They told me I would never make it, and that this network marketing thing wouldn't work for me.

"Maybe you're right, but the worst that can happen is that I'll have to come back and get a job like you've got," I replied. You could have heard a pin drop!

"The worst that can happen is I will have to come back and get a job like you've got."

There are a couple of negative people in this world and they move around a lot.

The Invisible Mountain

As a child, it was not until I started elementary school and faced the challenge of reading that I began to get beaten down. I had severe dyslexia and I could not read. No matter how hard I tried—and believe me, I tried—I could not read. All the words just ran together. The school's assumption was that I was slow, stupid or lazy. (Remember, this was long before dyslexia was identified as a disability.)

CHAPTER 3

My First Big Challenge

I often look back now and think of dyslexia as a mountain, an invisible mountain. I couldn't see it. My parents, my friends and my teachers had no idea about the challenge I faced. They assumed that I was just a dumb kid.

Why Can't John Read?

It was so very frustrating for me and for everyone around me. My parents took me to the eye doctor to see if I needed glasses. My vision wasn't as good as it could have been and I did get glasses, but I still couldn't read. The school tried different approaches to reading, even having me use a ruler with an open slot in it so I could see only one word at a time.

The frustration was not just mine. My teachers wanted to know why I could not read, my parents wanted to know why I could not read and I wanted to know why I could not read.

I Just Wanted to Be Invisible

As you can imagine, the feelings of inferiority were overwhelming. In some respects, I hold my teachers responsible. However, back then, they didn't know any better. They thought I was slow or stupid or simply not trying hard enough. When they called on me to read aloud in class, I stumbled through the sentences. The embarrassment I felt was unbelievable. Not only could I not read, but my classmates also taunted me.

When we read in class, we would each take turns reading a paragraph aloud. I used to count ahead to guess which paragraph I would be called on to read. I would practice and practice so I could somehow get through it. Then the teacher would go and call on someone out of order and mess me up completely. Imagine feeling as low as you have ever felt. That's how I felt every day at school. Imagine being called out of class during every test so that the test could be read to you.

My parents knew how good I was at building with my hands, but they were frustrated. I remember sitting in the garage one day and overhearing my dad tell one of his best friends how stupid I was and how he wondered what I was going to do in life. I crawled into the doghouse with my Black Lab,

Lady, and cried. (At least she understood me. If everyone had the same compassion and love that a dog has, we would live in a much better world.) Many such incidents occurred. The saddest part was that I started to believe that I was a slow, stupid kid. When that's all you hear, you begin to believe it to be true.

Ultimately, it was determined that I would never be able to read and that I should be taught what I needed to survive. I was placed in special classes and taught life basics such as balancing a checkbook, reading a menu, and learning to recognize street signs.

All through school, and even initially on the job, I wanted to be invisible. My self-esteem was so low that if I passed someone in the hallway, I wouldn't look up and say hello unless they spoke first. If people were laughing, I thought they were laughing at me. If people were talking, I thought they were talking about me. I wanted to float through life unnoticed.

I'm sure you can understand why my family was initially so against my going into network marketing. I'd spent my life avoiding people, and suddenly I wanted to get into the people business, the relationship business.

My experience has convinced me that if I can succeed in this business with my severe limitations and background, then anyone can do it. Looking back, I am reminded of a quote by Les Brown:

> *Many people want to tiptoe through life to get safely to death.*
>
> –Les Brown

CHAPTER 4

BACK TO THE STARTING LINE

Sometimes we all have to start over.

John, you were doing well at National Safety Associates (NSA). Why did you leave?

My four years working at NSA selling water filters was an excellent learning experience. I earned more money than I'd ever earned in my life. The first indication that there was a problem was when Jeff Olson, a major player, left.

For the first time, I took off my blinders and looked around. I realized that I hadn't heard of any new people who were making any money since I'd joined the business. Our superiors were still telling the same stories that I'd been told when I first got started. Jeff Olson made a strong case on the importance of timing.

Eventually NSA introduced a line of consumable products. They are a strong, growing company today.

Lessons Learned. I learned two very important lessons from my first network marketing experience.

The importance of a consumable product: Residual income is a huge benefit of network marketing. It means you can tell your story once and be paid over and over again, but this only works if your products are used every day.

The importance of timing: Timing is very, very important. I got involved with NSA just as it was moving into the end of its momentum. It seemed like everyone I talked to had heard of NSA and its water filters.

Why Do Some People Fail?

As I look back on my experience, I believe that there are three reasons why many people don't succeed in network marketing.

1. *It Takes Work*

The first reason is that many people don't apply themselves. It's called netWORKing. Just as with any business, you have to concentrate and work on it. If you invested $1 million in a McDonald's restaurant, would you just let it drift or would you be there first thing every morning and be the last to leave every night until it was a thriving business?

2. *They Were Too Late*

Network companies can reach a point of perceived saturation. Amway is a good example of this. It's difficult to run a successful business when everyone you approach about your products says, "Oh, I know about that. It's not for me."

3. *They Were Too Early*

Unfortunately, most start-up network marketing companies fail, with 95 percent failing in their first year, and only 2 percent making it to their fifth year. This is very sad because so many distributors have their hopes based on a "sure thing that cannot fail." But these companies do fail, and they take the hopes and dreams of their people down with them.

Picking the Right Company for You

Sometimes it takes a while to recognize the benefits and to realize what we have in network marketing. It may not be until you're with your second or third company that you understand the power of the business. Most people's first business experience comes when they join a company based on the enthusiastic urging of a friend. They have no understanding of the opportunity they have before them.

There are five critical elements that make up a successful opportunity.

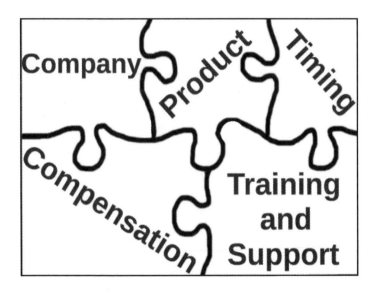

1. *Company*

The two most common reasons that companies fail are poor management and under-capitalization. The company must have a rock-solid infrastructure to accomplish success.

2. *Product or Service*

The product must be consumable, affordable, unique, and have a story that goes with it.

3. *Compensation*

Every company claims that they have the best, most lucrative compensation plan. The reality is that they all have the same money to pay out, between 40 and 50 percent of revenue. The real questions are, "Who gets the money?" and "What do you have to do to get it?" There are often many hurdles, "gotchas" that keep people from the money,.

4. *Timing*

Every company will tell you that their timing is perfect…right now. Timing is very predictable. It is a factor of numbers. There is a sweet spot in every company when it transitions from small into big. That is where you want to be.

5. *Training and Support*

There must be a proven training system in place, with tools that support that system. These tools must be affordable.

To get a better understanding of these elements, visit www.rightoralmostright.com.

My First Mentor – Jeff Roberti

One of my very best mentors was Jeff Roberti, the top distributor at NSA. He gave me the most incredible advice I've ever heard. No matter what the problem was, he would explain that the solution was to "talk to more people."

What if that didn't work?

"Talk to more people."

Jeff is one of the top earners in network marketing today. He has earned more than $50 million in his network marketing career, so I think his philosophy works.

> *"Talk to more people."*
> *"Okay. And what if that doesn't work?"*
> *"Talk to more people."*

How do you learn this business of network marketing?
How do you become a good network marketer?
How do you become a leader?

The secret is in the doing.

It is only by doing, taking the steps, doing your parties, making the calls, getting out your CD's or DVD's, mp3's, digitial photos, inviting to your organization's conference calls, doing 3-ways with your prospect and your up-line. That's how you learn to do this wonderful business.

> *Take the step, you'll have the power.*

CHAPTER 5

WHY NETWORK MARKETING?

Millions spent on:
✓ Celebrities
✓ Advertising

Millions spent on:
✓ Real People
✓ Real Results

Everyone does network marketing; they just don't get paid for it. Every time you tell a friend about a great movie or an incredible restaurant, you are engaging in network marketing. There is no force on the planet more persuasive than a friend telling a friend.

The Truth about Network Marketing

Who Do You Believe?

When shopping for products, do you believe the big-budget advertising or a high-paid celebrity who may have never used the product? Or do you believe your friend who tells you about a product from their own first-hand experience? You believe your friend of course.

What Is Network Marketing?

Network marketing is nothing more than another form of distribution.

In traditional retail distribution, at least 50 percent of the product's cost is used to cover advertising fees. This money is spent to get you to buy the product. But what value does it add to the product?

In network marketing, no money is spent on advertising.

Those (celebrity) funds are paid to real people using the products with real results.

The Benefits of Network Marketing

Product Quality

I'm convinced that you get a higher quality product from network marketing than you get from a retail store. Why? Every product in a retail store competes on price. The lowest price wins. What gets sacrificed? Quality!

Network marketing products are driven by results. You buy them because an acquaintance told you about their results with the product. Without results from quality products, network marketing does not thrive.

From my very first introduction to network marketing, over 25 years ago, to every party and event I go to today, I am constantly amazed at the product results people see.

Customer Service

The best example is a typical retail store such as Target, Home Depot or Walmart. There is very little customer service in most retail stores. There is usually no one to talk to and no one to answer your questions about a product.

Poor customer service is one of the most frustrating aspects of today's retail market. We have all made that call to ask a simple question. We go through the typical menu of recorded prompts, and when we finally reach a live human being they don't have an answer to our question, so they put us on hold and try to find someone with an answer. If we're lucky, we get an answer to our question, but don't bet on it.

Network marketing is all about customer service. Your sponsor, the leaders in your organization, and your company's customer service are only an e-mail or a phone call away with the answer to your question.

The Opportunity of a Lifetime

The most exciting part of network marketing is that it gives ordinary people the opportunity to build financial freedom. Network marketing is a level playing field. It has three requirements. First, you have to recognize it. Second, you have to take action. Third, you must have the desire to persist.

- ✓ Everyone has the same opportunity to succeed.

- ✓ Everyone starts equal, regardless of their education, age, financial position or background.

- ✓ You can start out part time.

- ✓ You can keep the security of your full-time job.

- ✓ You can go full time when you're ready.

- ✓ It has the potential of thousands of dollars part-time.

Network marketing is one of those very few opportunities that allow an ordinary person to pursue a second income and their dream of financial security and independence.

Tax Advantages

The tax advantages of network marketing alone can cover your start-up costs. You may be able to write off a percentage of your residence costs, your car, your travel and your product costs for sampling.

> *I was audited once and I had deducted 100 percent of both my vehicles. The revenue agent said, "It can't be all business. You must at least go to church on Sunday."*
>
> *I said, "Yes, but I pray for new distributors." He didn't buy my story.*

Better Reach

With network marketing, you can reach people that traditional retail will never reach. Typically you meet people in their homes and often through a CD or audio they play in their car or on a video they watch online

Leverage

Network marketing gives the ordinary individual an opportunity to use the same leverage that every business uses. A business leverages the time and talents of its employees to generate a profit. Network marketers leverage the time and talents of their distributors by helping them build business and income.

Residual Income

Network marketing is like writing a book, recording a song or drilling an oil well. You do the work once, but you get paid over and over and over for your efforts. I remember hearing a network marketing leader tell about driving across town one night to present their products. Their prospect signed up for an auto ship. Now, 20 years later they are still using the product and generating commissions.

How to Have a 40-Hour Day

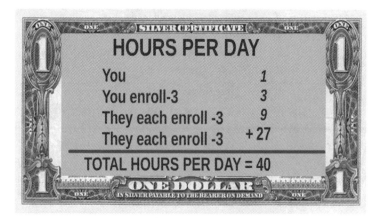

YOU NOW HAVE 40 PEOPLE WORKING 1 HOUR A DAY

THAT'S a 40-HOUR *DAY*— NOT a 40-HOUR WEEK

This is a simple illustration of forty people working one hour a day. You find three people, they find three people, and so on; but this illustration is only three levels deep. In reality, most companies pay eight to ten levels deep, so you can have thousands of people, worldwide, working that one hour a day.

Who's Making Money Off of Us?

I often hear people say, "The problem with network marketing is that someone is making money off of me." But isn't it also true that every time you spend money, someone is making money off of you? It's a cold, hard fact that 97 percent of people give their money to the 3 percent that own businesses. Every time you pay a bill, buy gas, buy groceries, or go out to dinner, someone is making money off you. This is just the nature of business. If a business does not generate an income, it is soon history.

Network marketing gives you the opportunity to participate in this cycle. Now you can be on the receiving end.

A friend of mine at The Barrel of Fun, said, "I don't like network marketing because someone is making money off me."

My response was, "I don't think they're losing money on us here. If someone is paying you $10 an hour, they must be making $15 to $20 an hour from your services. No one employs us to lose money."

Word of Mouth

What does the most famous ride in American history have to do with network marketing? Just about everyone knows about Paul Revere's ride and his message, "The British are coming!"

According to Malcolm Gladwell, Paul Revere's ride is the most famous historical example of a word-of-mouth epidemic. A piece of extraordinary news travelled a long distance in a very short time, mobilizing an entire region to arms.

Network marketing is a word-of-mouth business. Word-of-mouth, friend-to-friend is still the most important form of communication even in this age of mass communications and multi-million-dollar advertising campaigns. Think for a moment about the last expensive restaurant you went to, the last expensive piece of clothing you bought, and the last movie you saw. In how many of those cases was your decision about where to spend your money heavily influenced by the recommendation of a friend?

What Do the Experts Say?

There are many advertising executives who claim that word-of-mouth appeals have become the *only* kind of persuasion that most people respond to anymore.

Network marketing spends zero dollars ($0) on big-name actors, athletes and high-budget advertising campaigns. It doesn't spend millions on Tiger Woods or any other celebrity who might never use its products. Instead, those funds are given to real people who use the products with real results. You share your product experiences with your friends and in doing so you use the most effective real marketing on the planet—word of mouth, friend to friend, face to face.

To what extent do you trust the following forms of advertising?

Global Average	Trust Completely/ Somewhat	Don't Trust Much/ At All
Recommendation from people I know	92%	8%
Consumer opinions posted online	70%	30%
Editorial content such as newspaper articles	58%	42%
Branded Websites	58%	42%
Emails I signed up for	50%	50%
Ads on TV	47%	53%
Brand sponsorship	47%	53%
Ads in magazines	47%	53%
Billboards and other outdoor advertising	47%	53%
Ads in newspaper	46%	54%
Ads on radio	42%	58%
Ads before movies	41%	59%
TV program product placements	40%	60%
Ads served in search engine results	40%	60%
Online video ads	36%	64%
Ads on social networks	36%	64%
Online banner ads	33%	67%
Display ads on mobile devices	33%	67%
Text ads on mobile phones	29%	71%

Imagine buying a pair of shoes for $200. What is the real cost to make those shoes in China?

We know that the real cost of those shoes might be $5. That means as much as $100+ was spent on sponsorship by big-name sports celebrities. But did that $50 to $100 make the shoes better? Did it make them more durable or last longer?

The bottom line with all this is that network marketing is not just a better form of distribution with higher-quality products and incredible customer service, but it's an opportunity for an everyday person to live the American dream. You can go from ordinary to extraordinary. You can live a life beyond your wildest imagination just by showing others the opportunity. It's simple, but it's not easy. It takes time, persistence and a willingness to accept rejection. Not everyone you know is ready to change his or her life.

It's called *Net WORK* marketing.

The key word is **WORK**.

For more incredible statistics on network marketing and to also review the industry's scams, please visit www.rightoralmostright.com.

I have a dream.

One of the key skills of leadership is to get others to believe in themselves, to believe that there is a better way and to believe that they can win.

> *There's no business, no profession, no activity more noble than that of encouraging the development of people.*

You don't suddenly wake up one morning as a great network-marketing leader.
You don't suddenly realize that you have changed the lives of hundreds of people.

Greatness is earned one step at a time.

Greatness is found in the small step, in the moment of the decision to act.

Look back at the end of every day and ask yourself what small step to greatness did I take today?

CHAPTER 6

THE BIGGEST MISTAKES
WE ALL MAKE

John, you talk about doing the right things. What are some of the biggest mistakes that distributors make?

Almost Right: Spending time with the wrong people.
Right: Spending time with the right people.

Undoubtedly, the biggest mistake distributors make, not only when they're new distributors—but even after they've been in the business for a long time—is that they spend time with the wrong people. I still find myself falling into this trap. You can't push a rope.

How can you tell if that new distributor is the right person?

- ✓ They call you.

- ✓ They are on the conference calls.

- ✓ They have guests on a conference call.

- ✓ They have guests at an event.

- ✓ They attend all events.

- ✓ They are prospecting.

- ✓ They are coachable.

- ✓ They follow your company's system.

The bottom line is that they are doing the activities that will build their organization. You don't have to force them. It's just like fishing. If you have to ask, "Is this a big fish?" then it's not. You know you have a big fish when the rod is pinned to the rail and the fish is taking out line.

Some distributors want success more for their people than their people want it for themselves. Even so, I'm not suggesting that you forget anyone because everyone is important. Everyone counts, and you never know to whom they will lead you, but you must match energy with energy.

The saddest thing about spending time with the wrong people is that it distracts your attention away from prospecting, or looking for the right person. Network marketing is a business of sifting. The more you sift, the more likely you are to find your stars.

What makes a star?

Stars do the activities listed. They show initiative. They are actively doing the business.

The only way you will ever know you have a star is by the activities they do, never by what they say they will do. The sad fact is that when it's all said and done, there is more said than done. Don't get caught up in what they say, only in what they do.

John, I'm just so busy working this business.

Almost Right: Being busy all the time on the wrong activities.
Right: Focusing on "pay-time" activities.

Don't confuse activity with accomplishment. People often confuse activity, or being busy, with accomplishment. There you are, you're busy, busy, busy all the time, but are you really getting anything done? Don't confuse pay-time activity with no-pay-time activity. New distributors get paid for talking to someone who is not in the business. It may be someone you want to recruit on your front line, or it may be for someone in your down line, but as a new distributor you get paid only for talking to someone who is not in the business. Until you are earning $5,000 a month, 100 percent of your time should be spent on recruiting.

The skill to do comes in the doing.

Pay-Time versus No-Pay-Time

Pay-time is time spent talking to someone who is not in the business. No-pay-time is all the other activities you love, such as organizing your files, reading the literature, and watching the product video for the twelfth time. While it's all good stuff, it won't add a nickel to your next commission check.

The difference between a rich man and a poor man is how they spend their time.
–Robert Kiyosaki

Prepare Your List

John, I'm preparing my list, but I know only a few people who would be interested.

Almost Right: Handpicking those you think will do the business.
Right: Never, never, never prejudge.

Make two lists. The first list is those you think will be interested. The second list is those you think will not be interested. The second list will probably be the longer and more productive of your lists. You don't have the ability to know for certain who will be interested and who won't. You need to give everyone the opportunity to say no.

You may tell yourself, "This person makes too much money," or, "This person doesn't make enough money," or, "This person wouldn't be able to sell." Remember, you don't know who will be interested until you ask, and you never know who will be your superstar.

You can find a form to help you make your list, as well as some suggestions on building your business at www.rightoralmostright.com.

Would You…?

> *Would you have approached a shy, introverted*
> *maintenance manager with a severe learning disability*
> *who was living in a trailer park and deeply in debt?*
> *Would you have prospected me?*

No matter where you are, picture yourself as a 5 on a scale of 1 to 10. No matter how successful you have been, rank yourself as a 5. Now go out and talk to other people who would be ranked as 5 or higher.

All network marketers are tempted to recruit people who really need the business; those who have not been as successful as they have. You don't feel as uneasy when you approach them. But what happens when you start the trend this way? You talk to 4's, the 4's talk to 3's, the 3's talk to 2's, and before you know it you've got a group of couch potatoes. Always recruit up. The most successful distributors are those who recognize this principle.

> *It is not your job to judge anyone or to decide for anyone.*
> *It is your job to get information in front of anyone and*
> *everyone, and let them make their own decisions.*

Say Less to More People

Write this on a 3x5 card: "Say less to more people." Write it in your Day-Timer. Put it on the dashboard of your car. Write it on your mirror. Keep it in front of you. "Say less to more people." Stop talking before you're finished. We all talk too much. Read this phrase out loud and burn it into your memory.

Say less to more people.

Say less to more people.

Say less to more people.

Say less to more people.

Say less to more people.

One of the biggest challenges network marketers face, especially those who have experience in sales, is that they talk too much. Good communication is listening 70 percent of the time. Most people talk 70 percent of the time or more — much more. So, say less to more people.

Why is this important?

When you just keep talking, your prospects can't ask the questions they need to ask. Their questions tell you what they are thinking and how you can assure them. If you just keep talking, sooner or later you will bore them, and their only interest will be in getting away from you. Questions are magic! I love to ask questions such as, "Does that sound interesting? Is that something in which you're interested? Would you like to know more?"

If you talk too much:

- ✓ You will overwhelm them.

- ✓ If you don't ask questions you won't know what they need to know.

- ✓ If you come across as an expert, they will simply decide that they could never do that, and you've lost them.

- ✓ You will lose their attention. We all have short attention spans.

Your job is to answer questions, and the best way to do this is to direct them to a tool. A tool answers every question perfectly.

I'm getting a lot of interest through social media such as Facebook, but nobody is joining. What's wrong?

Almost Right: Introducing your business through social media and continuing to lead people to a decision through social media.
Right: Once people are interested, get them on the phone.

Social media is a great way to announce what you're doing. It's a great way to go public. The key is not to sell on social media, not to give too much information or attach a link. The goal is simply to create curiosity, to get someone to say, "It sounds exciting. Tell me more."

When someone responds to your social media, your number one objective must be to create rapport. You will never do this by telling them all about your product, your company or yourself. Find out about their interests. Ask questions such as:

✓ What are you interested in?

✓ What are you looking for?

✓ What attracted you to my post?

The end game is not to carry on lengthy back and forth communication. My best response is, "When can we talk?"

The average person has 300 friends on Facebook. Every time someone comments, Facebook alerts all of their friends. This is a great way to get your story out.

BUT...

Social media will never, never, never take the place of one motivated person telling a friend about what he or she has just learned. Network marketing is friend-to-friend marketing. When it comes down to getting someone to place an order, there must be a personal phone conversation.

I've got a lot of great ideas for how to build my business. How do I share these great ideas with everyone?

Almost Right: Trying new approaches to the business.
Right: Following a proven system.

This is all about following systems with NO shortcuts.

"Let's imagine that you're baking a cake. You have a recipe with steps and ingredients and you know it works. If you follow the recipe, you will have a great cake.

BUT if you decide to leave something out or skip a step, you end up with something, but it's not a cake."

–Andrea Gebhardt

Don't Reinvent the Wheel

Most companies have a proven system that works. If it's worked for thousands and thousands of other distributors, don't you think it will work for you too?

Not long ago, a guy came into my business with a sales background and told me, "John, you've done great, but I'm here now. I'll show you how this should be done."

My response was, "You know what, Joe, I've made millions doing it this way. Why don't we try it this way first?" Don't reinvent the wheel.

What works in network marketing today worked fifty years ago, and it will work fifty years from today. When someone tells you he has a new system, be very skeptical. If someone told you that he manufactured antiques, would you believe him?

There may be new techniques such as social media, but the fundamentals never change. Network marketing is a person-to-person, face-to-face sharing process.

DO YOU KNOW A KNOW-IT-ALL?

One of the reasons I believe that anyone who sets their mind to do this business can do it, is because if I can do it with my background, then you can do it with your background.

Network marketing is not about where you came from, it is about where you're going.

It's not about the color of your skin, what side of the tracks you were born on, your education, your age, your title, or your gender.

It's all about your determination to be all that you can be and to take the small steps to the TOP that will take you to your WHY.

CHAPTER 7

RIGHT OR ALMOST RIGHT

Frustration or celebration?
Struggling or thriving?
A little money or a lot of money?

This chapter is intended to introduce you to the Circle of Success. We all follow this circle no matter what our company or product. The question is, "Are we doing things right or almost right within the circle?"

In this chapter and on our website, www.rightoralmostright.com, there are examples of people who seem to be doing everything right. They certainly believe they're doing everything right, but they're not seeing the results they expect.

On the surface, and in their opinion, they are doing everything right but it's the small subtleties that make the difference between good and great.

- ✓ What's the difference between a good quarterback and a legend?

- ✓ What's the difference between a typical golfer and a great golfer?

- ✓ What's the difference between a good teacher and an excellent teacher? Both teachers have the same lesson plan and the same students, but one teacher seems to reach the students, while the other does not.

It's the small things that make the difference.

It's the twist of their wrist for the quarterback; it's the way they plant their feet for the golfer; it's their focus on the student for the teacher. These small things separate the average from the outstanding.

This section is all about doing the right things, and doing those things right.

John, are they doing it right or almost right?

I believe they're doing it almost right. It's the little subtleties that will make a big difference in the results you see. I absolutely believe that if you make these small changes, you'll get the results you're looking for.

The Circle of Success

Regardless of the company or product, the circle of success is the same. All network marketers go through these four steps on their way to success: Prepare yourself, share your story, follow up, and get a positive decision.

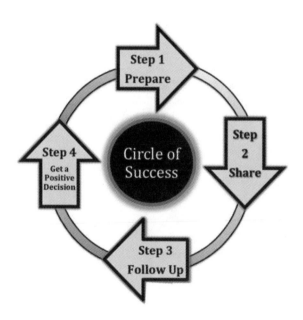

Over the course of the next four chapters, I'm going to go through the circle of success to illustrate the "right or almost right" process.

Why are you stepping?

Where are you stepping to?

The most important question is,

"What is MY top of the mountain?"

What is the top for you?...What excites you?

CHAPTER 8

PREPARE

People talk about being lucky. I believe that luck occurs when opportunity meets preparedness. Just as with anything that is accomplished in life, preparation is the cornerstone of success.

In this section, I will share with you what I believe to be "right" not "almost right."

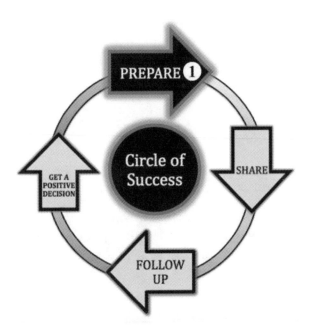

Prepare Your "Why"

> **Almost Right:** Getting your vision and your goals in writing.
> **Right:** Reviewing them morning and night.

Daily cultivation of your vision will stimulate your emotions, and trigger the creative juices in your mind that will lead to the achievement of your dream. Go through the following exercise several times a day.

Sit back with your eyes closed and picture what your life will be like when you arrive; when you achieve your "why." When you actually get there, it will be like déjà vu, because you've lived it over and over in your mind so often that it will seem familiar.

No matter who you are, you have to pay the price of success. It's hard to pay the price when the picture isn't clear, so you must have a clear picture—a vision of your "why." Daily cultivation is the only way to build your resolution into a burning passion.

> *As Earl Nightingale says in The Strangest Secret,*
> *"You are what you think about. If you can control your*
> *thoughts, you can control your destiny."*

New Year's Resolutions

Everyone knows this example. Many people make New Year's resolutions, but by late January or early February, those resolutions are long forgotten. Why? Were the resolution makers not serious when they made those resolutions? I believe they were quite serious.

BUT...

Without daily cultivation to build the resolution (the goal, the dream, the "why") into a burning passion, it will not succeed! There must be an emotion behind the motivation.

> *It's hard to pay the price*
> *when the picture is not clear.*

I'll give you another example to expand on this. I can still see this as clearly as I did on the day it happened. I was at a corporate conference, and a guy walked across the stage as a Triple Diamond, the top position. I will never forget what he said: "I was a Triple Diamond the day I signed up. It just took a while for the paperwork to catch up." That's the attitude. That's the winning mind-set.

That's the emotion behind the motivation.

Prepare Your Commitment

No one wants to follow someone who is not committed. Sticking your toe in the water doesn't work. You need to be basking in the pool, saying, "Come on in! The water's great!"

Commitment is the backbone, the foundation of success in every business. Commitment comes back to the fact that people buy people. People are not going to follow someone who is not committed. I'll give you a couple of examples.

I was in Minneapolis doing a two-on-one presentation with a brand-new distributor and a prospect. I did the presentation and the prospect became very excited. The prospect looked at the new distributor and said, "Well, Joe, this looks really good. What are you doing with it?"

Joe replied, "I'm between jobs. I thought I'd give it a try." You know what your response would be if you were that prospect?

"Try it on someone else, not me." People want to work with people who are committed, people who are focused and going places.

> *"Whatever the mind can conceive and believe it will achieve. You would not have had the thought if you were not capable of its accomplishment."*
> **–Napoleon Hill, *Think and Grow Rich***

Another example is in your own workplace. You can tell the people who are committed to their company and are there to do their job the best they can, versus the people who are there only to pick up a paycheck. No one has to tell you who is who. You can see it in his or her actions.

It's the same in network marketing. Commitment is very, very important. It's not easy to maintain your commitment when the tough times come—when you give out 25 CD's without a shred of interest, when the dream stealers get to you, or when you keep investing time and money with no return. As Earl Nightingale says, "It's hard to pay the price when the picture isn't clear."

Suppose I guarantee you $100,000. I put it in a bank account payable to you in twelve months. Your job, every week, is to get out three CD's, do three two-on-one meetings, and bring two people to a business presentation. Will you be committed? Without question, you would do it. You would be committed. You could see the picture, because it would be crystal clear.

Now, what if I told you that if you do the same things, you'll get double that amount? You'll get $200,000, but there is no guarantee. It will be more difficult for you because the picture isn't quite as clear.

Prepare Your Mind Set

One of the greatest challenges network marketers face in building the business is the emotional roller coaster. It's not a matter of, "Will you get knocked down." You will get knocked down. The question is, "Will you get back up?"

Knowing ahead of time that this will happen gives you the right mind-set to get back up.

Here are some tips for keeping the right mind-set:

- ✓ Stay plugged in to the calls and the events.

- ✓ Keep putting the good stuff into your mind. When you're in your car, working out, or enjoying some downtime, listen to your company audios and to personal development audios.

- ✓ Be ready for the dream stealers. Not everyone is going to buy your story. The important thing is that you don't buy their story about why it won't work.

With regard to the last tip, I remember trying to recruit an old friend in my hometown. He was completely negative. He gave me every reason in the world why the business wouldn't work, including, "The Chinese will come out with it, and you guys will be all done." He had a list of reasons a mile long.

I finally shut him up by saying, "If you were around when Thomas Edison was working on the light bulb, you would've talked him out of it, and we would all be reading by candlelight." I finished, "Even if my business ended tomorrow, I'd still be a million dollars ahead of you."

Don't expect everyone to believe your story. The important thing is that you don't let people convince you that their stories have merit. One of the reasons that your opportunity is so lucrative is because most people will not see it. It's very important to maintain a positive mindset. Do not let negative people or negative thoughts take your amazing opportunity away from you.

It's not important that everybody buys your story. It is important that you don't buy their story.

> *If it's hard, then do it hard.*
>
> **–Les Brown**

> *Execution is everything. Having just a vision is no solution; everything depends on execution.*
>
> **–Brian Tracy**

John, no one seems interested in my story.

Almost Right: You've rehearsed your story well.

Right: You tell your story with incredible energy, belief and commitment.

Remember, people buy people. If no one is interested, it's not a good story or you're not telling it with enough enthusiasm, passion and posture.

> *Get your story down cold so you can deliver it hot.*
> **–Dan Kinneson**

Your story is an important part of your success. You should be able to tell it in sixty seconds. When you first get started, it might be better to tell someone else's story until you have one of your own. (Hint: If your prospect's eyes glaze over as you're telling your story, then it is way too long. You're rambling.)

You absolutely must be excited. When I first entered this industry, I didn't know what I was talking about. Moreover, my prospects didn't know what I was talking about either, but they wanted to do the business anyway. They could feel my passion!

> *There are two types of people —*
> *those who brighten the room when they enter it,*
> *and those who brighten the room when they leave it.*

For example, you could have two people sharing exactly the same story. One simply tells the story. The other tells the story with the kind of energy and excitement that I'm talking about.

I promise you, there will be two different responses.

This business is full of amazing stories told in DVD's, CD's, parties, books, phone calls, conference calls and conversations that bring in the biggest names in the business.

Would you have given a CD to a maintenance manager living in a trailer park who had such a painfully low self-esteem that he would avoid saying "hello" unless you spoke first?

Whoever took that step changed my life forever and in turn has changed the lives of thousands of my associates.

CHAPTER 9

SHARE

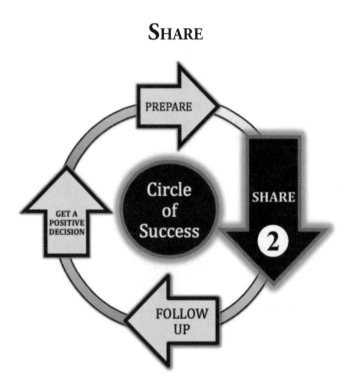

The essence of "share" is to **stimulate** an interest. It is not meant to **satisfy** that interest. The goal is to get your prospects to the next step, whatever that is. Perhaps it would be reviewing a tool or attending a home party/small group meeting.

It's like telling someone about a good movie or a great restaurant. You want them to want to learn more.

Sharing…Right or Almost Right?

Introducing Your Business

Your initial introduction should stimulate, not satisfy, interest. You want to give your prospects just enough to create intrigue so that they want to know more.

The danger you'll face, because you know so much, is that when prospects ask a question you'll want to answer them with a storehouse of information. I always respond with simple answers such as:

- ✓ "I just found out…"

- ✓ "We have to talk right away. When can we get together?"

- ✓ "Do you keep your income options open?"

- ✓ "Are you by your computer? You have to see this."

The concept is to create a sense of urgency and a fear of loss.

John, am I saying too much?

> **Almost Right:** Telling everybody, everything.
>
> **Right:** Listening more and talking less.

This is an area where I really caution people. This is a very common error with new distributors. They're so excited with the business, the products, the new vision, the compensation plan and the management team that they talk too much. In fact, they babble.

This can be done in every phase in the business, whether it's talking to a friend and blowing it by telling the whole story, talking too much on a three-way call when you're supposed to be listening, or overloading a poor prospect at a one-on-one presentation.

It's been said that 70 percent of communication is listening. Remember this the next time you get off on some long-winded explanation of the business: the one who does all the talking is the one who loses.

> *You will get knocked down.*
> *The question is, "Will you stay down?"*

John, as you go out today to sponsor more distributors, how do you go about it and what do you do?

Almost Right: Assuming that if you just give people the presentation, they will join.

Right: Understanding that recruiting is a process.

Once you sign on with network marketing, you expect that everyone will see the picture as soon as you explain it. You forget the process you went through in the beginning.

This process includes getting to know your people, and building belief, trust and rapport. Remember, they don't care how much you know until they know how much you care.

It typically takes three exposures to bring someone onboard. Recruiting, or bringing someone into the business, is not an event. It's a process, or a series of events, that leads to the individual saying, "Yes, count me in, or no, it's not right for me at this time in my life." Sponsoring is a process of exposure, or getting and keeping information in front of the prospect.

Your people will follow your example, so everything you do must be duplicable. They absolutely must feel comfortable doing what you do.

When Recruiting

Almost Right: Telling everyone everything *you* love about network marketing.

Right: Telling everyone how network marketing will work for *them*.

If someone says "no" to me I take it as a "not now." I keep them on my list and call them again in about 90 days. I keep the conversation very general by saying, "Just thought that I'd touch base and see how you're doing."

Every 90 days they become a new prospect. Their situation may have changed. Maybe they have lost their job, or maybe they are someplace different in their life. Maybe you've changed and you're better now.

John, I just love network marketing and I tell everyone I know how amazing it is.

Almost Right: Telling everyone everything *you* love about network marketing.

Right: Telling everyone how network marketing will work for *them.*

One of the first habits people fall into in network marketing is using the jargon of the industry. Up line, down line, cross line, sponsor, PV (personal volume), group, level, and organization mean nothing to a prospect. Using jargon will only cause confusion, and if your prospect is confused, he or she will never join your business.

Just tell them how they can get started part-time and not give up the security of their full-time job. Emphasize that they will be a member of a team that will support them. Be sure that they understand that when they say yes, that is when our job begins.

The skill to do comes in the doing.

The illustration below shows how fast communication moves today and just how powerful social media has become. Keep in mind that the 1.3 billion users described are those on Facebook (the number doesn't include other social media sites such as Twitter, Linked In, You Tube, Instagram, Pintercrest, etc.).

Social media is a great way to get your message out and to communicate. It plays a big role, and is, in fact, a must in the network marketing industry. That being said, social media will not get someone to say yes and join you. It is simply a way to stimulate interest and assist in the process of building belief.

To get others to join your business, you absolutely must talk to them on the phone.

radio	television	internet	social
38 Yrs To Reach	13 Yrs To Reach	4 Yrs To Reach	9 Months To Reach
50 Million	**50 Million**	**50 Million**	**100 Million**

How many people use Facebook:
1.393 billion monthly active users
Time spent on Facebook per user per day:
21 minutes

When someone expresses an interest on any social media, your response must be, *"When can we talk?"* Don't make the mistake of trying to satisfy their interest over social media.

NOTE: Young people (millennials) tend to ignore phone calls. They text first. If an older person calls them, they will often ignore the call, then text them back, 'what do you want?' Texting has changed the way younger people communicate.

John, I feel like I don't know enough.

> **Almost Right:** Thinking you need to know more.
>
> **Right:** Not needing to know it all. You'll learn as you earn.

Another mistake network marketers make is thinking that they need to know everything. Knowledge does not generate activity. Activity generates knowledge.

People learn by doing. Some distributors enter this business, particularly from the sales world, and think that they need to know everything—the ins and outs of the compensation plan and everything about the products. The problem is that everything you do in this business sets an example for how and what your people will do. If you go out there and talk like a product expert or a compensation expert, your people will think they have to be experts. You may impress them, and they may decide that they could never do what you do or know as much as you know.

Everything you do in the process of recruiting sets an example. It shows your people what they have to do to be successful.

> *You learned everything you need to know to be successful in network marketing in kindergarten.*
> *It's called Show and Tell.*

Remember the four SW's:
SW – SW – SW – SW – Next
Some will – Some won't – So what – Some waiting –

John, if someone asks me a question, why shouldn't I answer it?

When you share your business or product with someone, remember that your goal is to stimulate interest, not to satisfy interest.

The mistake many network marketers make is that when people start asking questions, they assume, wow, they are really interested, and they start answering their questions and giving them way too much information.

When people ask you a question, what they are really doing is trying to get enough information to see if this is something they have an interest in knowing more about. Do they want to spend the time to review your tool or come to your home party/small group presentation?

What typically happens is that they decide, based on a small fraction of the information, whether the business is for them, instead of reviewing the tool or attending your event and getting the whole story.

> *The key thing is to get started, to get going now.*

John, what do I do when someone says, "I'll look at yours if you'll look at mine?"

Almost Right: Okay, show me yours.

Right: I'm not interested in yours, but you need to look at mine.

This approach might have worked in kindergarten, but it doesn't work when you're talking to prospects. If you agree to the prospect's suggestion, then the whole time they're presenting their business, you're thinking how to refute it and show that yours is better. They are thinking the same thing when you're presenting your business.

When you meet people, you're always buying or selling. You're buying their story or you're selling your story. The right response, and this takes practice, is to say, "I'm not interested in what you have, but you have to see what I'm doing." You have to show that you're totally committed to your business.

Whoever demonstrates the highest level of commitment and belief will have influence over the other.

Earl Nightingale said that "success is the progressive realization of a worthy ideal or goal."

Progressive tells me that it is a process; it does not come all at once in some great quantum leap.

Success is progressive; it comes one step at a time.

Success. The choice always is yours.

CHAPTER 10

FOLLOW-UP

Follow-up to build belief must be done on a timely basis. If too much time elapses, you're always starting over. Remember, the fortune is in the follow-up.

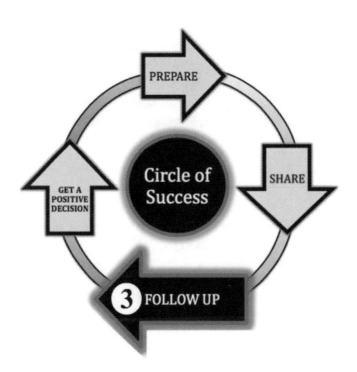

John, what is the best way ...

Almost Right: Invite by Facebook, posting links to your website, postcards, flyers, email.

Right: You can send a text to get their attention, then follow up. A live, personal call is the only way to invite and always get a firm commitment.

The most important aspect of a successful event is the attendance. Don't take the easy way out in the inviting process…pick up your phone.

John, what's the very best way to launch my new business?

To launch your business, there is nothing, absolutely nothing, better than a *party*. If done correctly, you will gather a group that can generate a lot of excitement. Here are some important points in doing it right:

✓ Do it as soon as possible, ideally within your new member's first seven to ten days of joining. Set the date, stick with it, and don't cancel.

✓ Invite properly. Without proper invitations, you won't have a successful party. Attendance is the most important thing. Without it, you don't have a party. The keys to inviting are that it absolutely must be done by phone and you need to get a firm commitment. Those who say "maybe" or "I'll try" will not be at your party. A good confirming question is, "Can I count on you?" You are looking for a firm yes.

✓ Do not invite too far in advance. Three days prior to your party is best.

✓ Warning: Inviting someone via Facebook, e-mail or a written invitation WILL NOT WORK. These types of invitations can be used in conjunction with your phone call to reinforce your invitation and to give the details, but they cannot take the place of your personal phone call.

✓ Be sure to confirm (via a phone call) the day of your party.

In terms of the home party itself:

- ✓ Start on time.

- ✓ Be sure the room is cool and comfortable.

- ✓ Remove all distractions such as pets and children.

- ✓ Be attentive. No sidebar conversations.

Most companies have a home party plan. Be sure you know yours and follow it.

What tools do you recommend in the follow-up process?

Remember, the goal is not just to use the right tool, but also to position the tool so your prospects review the information. If you have not stimulated an interest, most likely the prospects will not review the tool.

The Internet is a great way to get information to people, especially when they are long distance. Websites, YouTube, online videos, and online brochures provide excellent access to such information.

In addition, the energy and excitement that can come from a live webinar, conference call, or three-way call is powerful. The best way to get someone on a conference call is to three-way them on. Getting your prospect to attend a live local event is also greatly beneficial.

My personal favorite is an audio CD. It's a great way to build belief and reinforce your message. The key is to get your prospect to listen to the audio while they're in their vehicle. The same information may be available online, but most people have short attention spans when they're on the internet. When they are on the internet they're typically multi-tasking, with the TV on, the phone ringing and the family around. In the car, you have their undivided attention.

I keep telling my story, but no one gets back to me.

> **Almost Right:** Assuming people will get back to you.
>
> **Right:** Following up within 24 hours.

If you're not getting responses, the three most likely reasons are:

- ✓ You're talking too much. Remember, your goal is to stimulate interest so people want to know more.

- ✓ You need to remind yourself again that people buy people.

- ✓ Are you excited?

- ✓ Are you demonstrating your commitment and belief?

- ✓ You're not creating a sense of urgency and a fear of loss. The sense of urgency and fear of loss that I'm referring to should be similar to what you'd feel if you had rock-solid inside information on a penny stock that you knew was going to a dollar a share. How can you convey these feelings?

Follow up within 24 hours…Remember the fortune is in the follow up

John, I've been introducing my business to a lot of people, but I'm not getting much of a response.

> **Almost Right:** Talking to everyone you meet.
>
> **Right:** Following up within 24 hours.

The fortune is in the follow-up. There is absolutely no alternative to consistent follow-up. You have to follow up with your prospect within twenty-four hours. The best time to set up your follow-up is when you introduce your prospect to the business with a CD or DVD, or when you ask him to check out a website.

Get his permission with a specific time. For example, "Bob, I'd like to get your feedback. I'll call you tomorrow night around seven. Is that okay?"

They may not have done what they said they would. When you follow up, 50 percent of the time, they will not have visited the website or listened to the CD. Ask them when they'll have time and then set up a time with them to follow up again.

Remember, if you're not following up on a consistent basis, you're always starting over.

Follow up within 24 hours

Remember the fortune is in the follow up.

I keep hearing about three-way calls. Why is a three-way call so important?

Almost Right: Not doing three-way calls in every case.

Right: Doing a three-way call with every interested prospect.

Many times, you might feel like the prospect is not worthy, or that you can handle it on your own and don't want to bother your up line. The problem is that if you don't do three-way calls with your prospects, they won't do three-ways with their prospects. This breaks a critical step in the duplication process.

3rd Party Calling & Edification

You

Edification
Successful
Knowledgeable
Helpful
Fun

Trust
via Friendship

Respect
via Edification

Expert

Your Prospect

Benefits of a Three-Way Call

1. A third-party source always sounds more credible.

2. It's a learning experience for you. As your up line answers the questions, overcomes objections, and leads your prospects to a decision, all that information passes through your ears into their ears. It's the absolute best way to learn the subtleties of the business.

3. It builds belief in your prospects and in yourself as you hear the information again and again.

4. It demonstrates support to your prospects. They then see that they're not alone and there is someone to help them get going.

Will I be comfortable with my first few three-way calls?

Absolutely not! Most people are reluctant to do three-ways at first. Over time, as you see the value they bring, and how essential they are, you will come to believe in them.

I really like the idea of a three-way call.

What's the best way to do one?

Almost Right: Asking your prospects if they would be open to doing a three-way call.

Right: Having your up line on the phone when you call.

If you try to schedule a three-way with your prospects, most people will say no. They don't want to talk to someone they don't know. They're afraid of being pressured into something they don't want to do.

The best way to do a three-way call is to have your up line leader on the phone when you're doing your follow-up calls with the prospect. For example, "Hey, Bob, I'm following up on our conversation, and I have my friend Sally on the line. Sally's been in the business longer than I have, so she knows it better." Then be quiet and let Sally talk. Or, "I'm following up as I said I would. I'm new myself, and I thought you might have some questions. I was talking to Sally, the person I'm working with, who has more time in the business, and has had great success. I hope you don't mind that I have her holding on the line." Then be quiet and let Sally talk.

When I'm Taking Those Small Steps To The Top Will There Be Any Obstacles?

Of course not…**if you live in a perfect world.**

The question is not, "Will there be obstacles?," or "Will I get knocked down?"

You will get knocked down.

The right question is, "Will you get up?"

If you find a series of steps with no obstacles, they probably don't lead anywhere.

CHAPTER 11

GETTING A POSITIVE DECISION AND OVERCOMING OBJECTIONS

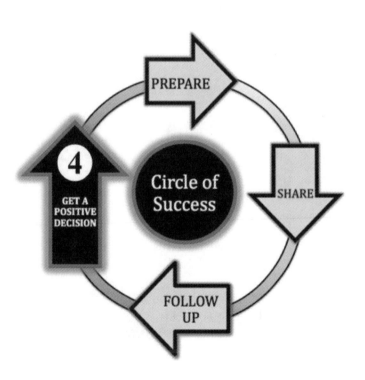

The Psychology of a Decision

If a prospect is just looking to buy your product it's an easy decision, no more difficult than buying groceries. The decision to join a business is far more complex. Whether you or the prospect realizes it, these are the things the prospect is thinking about.

Fear of failure and rejection. – What if it doesn't work? What will my friends and family think?

The key here is building their belief. Before someone will say "yes" to you, they must say "I can" to themselves. Part of helping someone build belief is showing them that their sponsor, their up line, their leaders, and the company are all there to support them and that many others have done it. They need to understand that when they say yes, that's when our job begins.

Do I have the time for it? – I'm so busy right now.

Most people are working very hard just to make ends meet. The sad thing is that they are working hard to build someone else's dream, someone else's security. I explain this to them, and ask if they could dedicate just one hour a day to build their own financial security. I explain that they may have to sacrifice something they love to do, like watching TV, or bowling, or playing a sport. I ask if they are willing to make that sacrifice to build their dream.

The cost – can I afford it? This is the easiest objection to overcome.

If you can show them how they can get their money back, their hesitancy to invest goes away. Help them see and understand and truly believe that they will get their money back by selling product or enrolling people.

*****

John, what is the best way to get a yes?

Almost Right: You've shared everything with your prospect, and they should be ready to get started.

Right: ASK them to get started.

The essence of getting a positive decision is to ask for one. Please note: You want your prospects to say yes, but what your prospects need to say to themselves before they will say yes to you is, "I can do this."

A common mistake network marketers make is to keep giving information until someone finally says, "Yes, I'm ready to get started." One of the most difficult things to do is to ask for the order—to ask for money.

The million-dollar question is, "Do you see an opportunity for yourself with this?"

- ✓ If NO: "Which products are you interested in trying?"

- ✓ If UNSURE: "What questions do you have?" Listen to their answer and then ask, "Do you see this as an opportunity for yourself?"

- ✓ If YES: Reach for the application and help them complete it immediately.

When someone can't say no, but they also can't seem to say yes, what do you do?

Almost Right: Keep going over and over the same information.

Right: Find out what's holding them back.

When people are interested, but not sure, it means one or more of the following:

✓ They do not understand something.

✓ They have questions.

✓ They don't know if they can do it.

✓ Their belief is not there yet.

✓ They are afraid they will fail.

The key is to find out what is holding them back. I like to ask, "On a scale of one to ten, with ten being ready to get started, where are you?"

If they say, "Seven," then I ask, "What else do you need to know to move to a ten?"

Sometimes people just don't know what's holding them back. In this case, they may be afraid, and you'll need to assure them that even though they will be in business for themselves, they will not be alone.

They need to know when they say yes, that's when your job begins. One of my favorite techniques, in this case, is the "Ben Franklin" approach of listing out the pros and cons. Ben took a page and drew a line down the center. He then listed the pros on one side and the cons on the other side.

The key to this approach is to make a shared commitment up front, that no matter what, they will do whatever the comparison indicates.

Pros	Cons
· Own your own business · Time freedom · Tax benefits · Work from home · No commute · Leveraged income · Residual income · Low risk · Own your own life · Work on your dream	

I always help my prospects with the pros and let them fill in the cons themselves. In every case, the picture is very clear.

What's the best way to overcome an objection?

Almost Right: Point out why the objection is not valid. You end up arguing.
Right: Right is *feel...felt...found.*

A common mistake network marketers make is that when they're faced with an objection, they end up arguing. When this occurs, your prospects' defenses come up and they shut down on you. As Stephen Covey says, "Seek first to understand and then to be understood."

My all-time best response comes when I use the words feel, felt, and found. Rather than argue with them, agree with them. Say, "I know how you feel." This completely disarms them and lowers their barriers. They cannot argue with someone who agrees with them. Then say, "I felt the same way." Now you're empathizing with them. They're thinking that you're just like them, and that you understand. This opens them up to what you've found out. Then, you can say, "This is what I've found out." Now they're all ears, and curious to know what you've learned. You'll find this approach works in virtually every case.

Everyone says, "This looks real, but I just don't have the time."

Almost Right: Tell them it doesn't take much time.

Right: Use *feel…felt…found.*

Use *feel, felt,* and *found* again. "I know how you *feel*," or "I *felt* the same about it when I was introduced," or "Here's what I've *found.*" For example:

- ✓ "I've found that, because of leverage, this business actually gives me more time."

- ✓ "I've found that if I don't do something different, I will never have the time."

- ✓ "I've found that I could make the time, if I were convinced it was worth my time."

It looks like all you do is sign up people. Who sells the product?

Almost Right: We all sell the product.

Right: Use *feel…felt…found.*

I know how you feel. I felt the same about it when I was introduced. What I found out was that it's not a matter of who sells the product. The real question is about who uses the product?

If you become a customer, I sell you the product, you use it, and I make a few dollars. If I sign you up, you become a distributor, you're still using the product, and you're sharing it with others who use the product whether they sign up or simply become customers. But by signing you up, it goes from just you using the product to possibly hundreds, and maybe even thousands of people using the product.

The key is that the products are being used by somebody.

What do you say when people tell you, "I know someone who tried this and it didn't work?"

> **Almost Right:** Maybe he or she didn't really work at it.
>
> **Right:** Use *feel…felt…found.*

I know how you feel. I felt the same about it when I was introduced. Here's what I found out. I found that nothing works for everyone. I know people who failed in high school. It doesn't mean that high school doesn't work; it simply means it didn't work for those people.

In another example, 90 percent of real estate agents don't renew their license after the first year, and 95 percent of insurance agents fail within three years. These are agents who invested in schooling and training, and had to pass a test to do business.

In network marketing, if you can fog a mirror, you can sign up. The difference between network marketers and the agents above is that when people go to work for New York Life or Re-Max and it doesn't work, they don't go around saying it was a scam. They just recognize that the business was not for them, but when someone fails in network marketing, they say it was a scam. They don't take responsibility or acknowledge that they didn't work it well.

What do I say when people ask, "Is this a pyramid?"

> **Almost Right:** Say, "It's not a pyramid. Pyramids are illegal."
>
> **Right:** Ask them, "What's a pyramid?"

By answering a question with a question, it gives you the opportunity to get a deeper understanding of what they're thinking. In most cases, they will give an answer such as, "Well, you know, where the guy at the top makes all the money and the people at the bottom have no chance to get to the top."

Or they can't tell you what they really mean, so you ask, "Do you mean one of those things where the guy at the top makes all the money and the people at the bottom have no chance to get to the top?" In either case, you say, "No, it's not like that at all, but I used to work for one."

When I was a maintenance person at the Barrel of Fun potato chip plant, it was unlikely that I would ever be at the top of that corporate pyramid. In any corporation, for someone to move up, someone else has to move up or out. A corporation is structured far more like a pyramid than any network marketing company. In a corporation, or an actual pyramid such as a Ponzi scheme or chain letter, there is room for only one person at the top.

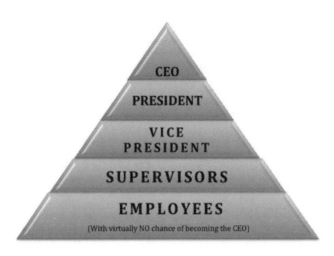

"NO thanks! Looks like a pyramid scheme!"

"This is what a real network marketing looks like"

Network marketing is actually an inverted pyramid. All the room is at the top and anyone can access it; however, most people won't do what it takes to get to the top.

What do I say when people say, "I have no money?"

Almost Right: You agree with them.
Right: You use this example.

Occasionally, you'll run into people who say, "I'm your person. I can do this business, but I have no money. I can't even do the basic level."

I'm a very firm believer that where there's a will, there's a way. If people truly want to do something, they'll figure out how to do it. I also believe that if people can't come up with the minimum investment, they will never make it anyway.

When a prospect tells me he doesn't have the money, I respond, "You're telling me that you can't come up with a few hundred dollars, but that you'll work your tail off to go after this, and that you'll be my star?" Then I ask him a question. I say, "Let's say that when we're finished talking here today, you leave and someone has vandalized your car. They've slit all four tires. What are you going to do? You're not going to walk everywhere you go. You're going to get new tires. Somehow, you'll find a way to buy those tires." I finish, "Here's the good news: your tires are fine. Wherever you would have found the money to buy those tires, that's where you can get the money so you can get started."

I've introduced my business to a lot of people. They walk away, saying, "It sounds good, but I can't do the business." What do you say to people like that?

Almost Right: Just let them go.
Right: Ask them, "If you were to do the business, why would you do it?"

When people say, "I can't do the business," challenge them with, "Let's be honest with each other. Everyone can do the business. You can do the business."

In many cases, prospects don't have a strong enough "why." The very first question I always ask interested prospects is, "If you were to do the business, why would you do it?" If they don't have a "why," you might as well move on. They also need to put a specific figure down on paper. Your next question should be, "If you were to earn this amount of money, what would you do with it? How would it change your life?"

Their answer may be, "I want my wife to be able to stay home," or, "I want to build a college fund for my kids," or, "I want to build a retirement fund," or, "I want to support my church." No matter the answer, they need to put it down on paper.

This is one of the most frequent responses I get: "Let me try the product, and then if I like it, I'll do the business." How would you respond?

Almost Right: Say, "Fantastic," and get them the product.
Right: Say, "Sounds great, but let me ask you…"

This is probably the most frequent response network marketers receive. Of course, you want people to use your products, but not to see if the products work. The products work. They do what they're supposed to do. The objective in using the products is to find out what works for you, and to become familiar with the rest. A product does not have the same effect for everyone who uses it.

Let's look at a few examples. People will say, "If these products work, then I'll be all over it."

My response is, "Well, what happens if they don't work for you? Nothing works for everyone. It doesn't invalidate the opportunity just because it doesn't work for you." The real product is the opportunity. You're selling hope. You're giving people a chance to free themselves from dead-end jobs.

The key should not be that if the product works, then your prospect will do the business. The key should be whether the product works for most people. That is the real the issue.

I get all kinds of reasons why prospects can't do the business.

People will come up with the most amazing excuses why they can't do the business. When I was building my NSA business, I was driving from my hometown of Perham to Fargo every morning, an hour-and-a-half drive. I was the first one to open the office door in the morning and the last one to leave at night. I was working with a young guy who was very enthusiastic. He lived in Fargo, but on the other side of town. Now the other side of Fargo is not like the other side of a major city. I'm talking ten to fifteen minutes away on a bad day. He was complaining to me about having to drive across town. Here I was driving seventy miles to be there early in the morning, every morning regardless of the weather, and he was complaining about driving across town.

It amazes me when people say they want something, yet they make excuses for why they can't get it. When one's heart is not in it, any excuse will do. It's like the man who asked his neighbor if he could borrow his lawn mower. The neighbor said, "No, I'm sorry. You can't borrow my lawn mower. My wife's making beef stroganoff."

The man asked, "What does beef stroganoff have to do with my borrowing your lawn mower?"

The neighbor responded, "Listen, if I don't want to lend you my lawn mower, one excuse is as good as another."

Some people look for an excuse. Winners look at every problem as a challenge. They find a way around it, either through it or over it. It gets under my skin when I see people complain about little things that mean nothing at all in the big scheme of life.

> *Whoever does all the talking loses.*

Whose Dream Did You Build Today?

CHAPTER 12

BUILDING YOUR BUSINESS

Brick ... by brick ... by brick ......

> *If the desire is strong enough,*
> *you can always find a way.*

Your DMO (Daily Method of Operation)

Your DMO is your routine. It should be as natural as brushing your teeth and combing your hair.

**Everyone has a Daily Method of Operation.
You do it with out even thinking about it!**

**Now you need to apply the System as
your Daily Method of Operation.**

- ✓ **Use the Product**
- ✓ **Share the Products/Opportunity**
- ✓ **Follow Up**
- ✓ **Support People**
- ✓ **Personal Development**

Time is our most valuable asset, yet we tend to waste it, kill it, and spend it rather than invest it.

–Jim Rohn

Time Management

Put your day on paper before it starts. When you put your day on paper, it helps you understand and focus on your priorities, AND you can look back at the end of the day and evaluate how many seeds you planted.

There is an old story about Andrew Carnegie, who was one of the great steel magnates. Like so many of us, Carnegie felt overwhelmed with all the things he had to do every day. Feeling very frustrated, he hired a consultant.

The consultant sat in Carnegie's richly paneled office with its high ceilings, floor-to-ceiling windows, and beautiful cherry oak desk and furniture and wondered what advice he could possibly give to this very successful business leader. As he thought through Carnegie's frustration at dealing with his everyday workload, he said, "Take a yellow pad, write down everything you have to do today and prioritize it. Now do the most important thing first. Do not move on to the next item on the list until it is completed, or you have done all you could have. By following this process, even if you don't get everything done, you will have accomplished at least the most important things."

Carnegie thanked him and asked how much he owed him. The consultant said, "Why don't you put the idea to work for a few weeks, and then send me a check for whatever you think it was worth." As the story goes, Carnegie sent him a check for $25,000. (This was when $25,000 was worth at least $250,000 in today's dollars.)

How does this story apply to the everyday network marketer? Most work this business part-time. Their lives are busy, and on many days they just don't get to their business, or, if they do get to it, they end up doing the things that are fun and easy.

Good time management

- ✓ Put your day on paper before it starts.

- ✓ Be aware of Pay Time vs No Pay Time.

- ✓ Know your priorities for the day.

Ask yourself (every day)

- ✓ What is most important today?

- ✓ How can I talk to more people?

My $25,000 Advice on Time Management

If you put your day on paper before it starts, it will be like taking a ton of bricks off your back. It will eliminate that sense of being overwhelmed.

Know the difference between pay-time and no-pay-time. This is especially true if you're working part-time. I've been told by so many people that they spend a lot of time building their business. When I ask them what they're doing, it turns out that they're doing no-pay-time activities.

Pay-Time

Focus your time on pay-time activities. You get paid for talking to people who are not using your products. Nothing is more important than carving out an hour or two every day to focus on pay-time.

Prioritize

The biggest mistake network marketers make in how they spend their time is that they don't prioritize.

Interruptions

Never let anything interrupt the time you set aside to build your business. This is your business, your new life that you're building. What interruption is more important than that?

Three Stages in Network Marketing

There are three stages you go through in network marketing.

In Stage I, you'll be underpaid. You'll have very little leverage and you'll be looking for your leaders and beginning to build your team. Most of your income will be from your own personal efforts. It's tough to get through that first underpaid stage. The first $5,000 you earn in this business will be the toughest $5,000 you will ever earn. You have to hold the vision and continue to move forward.

In Stage II, you'll begin to feel that you're being paid what you're worth. Your team will be growing and your leveraged income will begin to kick in. Your income will no longer be based solely on your efforts.

In Stage III, you'll be paid far more. Your business has a life of its own. It grows without you. Very little of your income is based on your own direct efforts.

TIME VERSUS MONEY

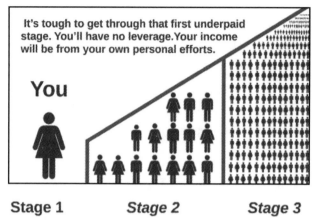

Over time you leverage more people and get paid more than your worth!

Remember this is a relationship business.

To really build and sustain an organization it's all about relationships.

✓ It's all about how much you care

✓ It's all about how you make people feel

✓ It's all about how you treat people

✓ Keep them in one more day and you may keep them for a lifetime

✓ Everyone counts regardless if they are full time going Mach II with their hair on fire or a very part timer

✓ People want to be valued, recognized and appreciated

John, I just enrolled a new member. What do I do now?

> **Almost Right:** Merely enrolling them in your business.
> **Right:** Getting them started right.

When people say yes to your business, that's when your real work begins. Think of yourself as their life support system. Remember that when you get people started, their excitement level is high but their knowledge is low. They are fragile. They are in the faith stage. You need to get them from faith, to belief, to passion.

Once you sponsor people into the business, take them through the "getting started" process. Be sure that they know who their up line leaders are, and that they have their phone numbers. Get them plugged in. Be sure they know about the conference calls. Help them get their list together.

I always say that there are two ways to get started, fast and slow. Fast is always better. You want to get a big check in their pocket as soon as possible. An excited person attracts others. If you do this, everything else will fall in place.

> *Leaders are like eagles; they don't flock together,*
> *you have to find them one at a time.*

*If you follow a script, you will be more effective.
Your distributors will follow a script, and they will be
more effective. Do you have a better idea?*

How many people will I have to approach to find my key leaders who will follow through and build the business?

Almost Right: Deciding that your last recruit is the answer to your prayers and putting all your efforts into that person. **Right:** Supporting everyone on your team AND recruiting every day. A star becomes visible very quickly.

I don't know the answer to that. Network marketing is like a bucket of oysters. You have to keep shucking the oysters until you find the pearls. Sometimes you find them at the top of the bucket, sometimes in the middle, sometimes at the bottom, and occasionally you have to get another bucket.

I can promise you this though—the pearls are there. They are always there. I know a lot of people who have quit, but I've never met anyone who failed. If you stay the course, and if you continue shucking oysters, you're going to find your pearls.

Ask yourself this question, "If I keep on doing what I'm doing, will it make my dream my reality?"

Finding Your Pearls in a Bucket of Oysters

What lies behind you, and what lies ahead of you
is of very little importance
when compared with what lies within you.

– Oliver Wendell Holmes

How do you know when you've got the right person to invest your time and energy in?

Almost Right: You think that he or she is the right person.
Right: He or she is doing the right things.

You may think that a person is your next star because he or she is sharp, well dressed, well connected, and so well spoken. The person looks the part! But if you have to ask yourself if he or she is the right person, that should be an alert for you. If you have to call to see if he or she will be on a call or at an event, that person is not going to be your star. You should be encouraging anyway, but he or she is probably not the right person.

It's like fishing. If you have a fish on the line and you're wondering if it's is a big fish. It's not. If it's a big fish, it's taking out the line and the rod is pinned to the rail.

When you're working with someone, and they are always calling you, and always have people for you to talk to, then you've got the right person.

I feel as if I'm all alone.

Almost Right: You don't want to bother your sponsor or your up line.
Right: You're using your sponsor and your up line.

In network marketing, you're in business for yourself, but not by yourself. If you're not using your up line leaders, then you're squandering an invaluable free resource. Your up line leaders have a vested interest, and a personal interest in your success.

Lone rangers lose. This business is not like the old movies where the Lone Ranger rides into town, shoots all the bad guys, cleans up the town, rescues the lady in distress and rides off into the sunset. In network marketing, the lone rangers lose. Your up line is there to be used. They are paid to help you be successful. Think of them as successful consultants, available on demand, at no cost to you. Your sponsor wants to hear from you. If your sponsor doesn't hear from you, he or she will assume that you're not doing the business. This is a business of team effort. You must employ the team, because you'll never be able to build a large organization without help, or without having your up line work with you.

It seems as if I'm working the business, putting in the time, but it's just not happening.

> **Almost Right:** Keep doing what you're doing, and it will happen.
> **Right:** Do a personal check up.

One of the things I always ask myself is, "What could I have done better?" If you feel that you're doing everything right and you're still not having the results you expected, you're probably doing the business "not right but almost right."

Do a personal evaluation in these areas:

- ✓ Your story. Are you rambling, are you excited, are you showing commitment?

- ✓ Are you spending time with the right people, or are you pushing a rope?

- ✓ Are you following a system, or are you using your own system?

- ✓ Are you spending your time on pay-time activities or non-pay-time activities?

- ✓ Are you setting the right example for your team? Are you doing the things you want them to do?

These are the types of questions you ask yourself, and then make whatever changes are necessary.

John, I keep doing the business, focusing on prospecting and helping my team, but it seems to go nowhere.

Almost Right: Focusing on the results you're seeing.
Right: Focusing on the seeds you're sowing.

Use the 90/10 rule. I learned this rule from an Amway Crown Ambassador while on a flight. I asked the ambassador, "Can you give me one piece of advice?"

The Crown Ambassador said, "Understand that 90 percent of everything we do, the money we invest, and the time we spend is wasted. It's the 10 percent that will make us wealthy beyond our dreams. The problem is that we don't know what the 90 percent is and what the 10 percent is, so we have to do it all."

The next time you're frustrated, remember the 90/10 rule. You're doing a meeting, but no one showed up. You travelled across town to meet someone, but they didn't show up. They didn't call to cancel, and then they didn't even apologize afterward. One of your key leaders quits the business, and you had your heart set on what that person could do. These are all part of the 90 percent. If you keep on doing the right things, they will include the 10 percent that will make you wealthy beyond your dreams.

Using this rule, 90 percent of what you do is totally wasted, while 10 percent of what you do makes you wealthy beyond your wildest dreams. If only you could know what is the 10 percent and what is the 90 percent!

It's important to understand that, for most people, success is not immediate. It takes a long-term commitment. When I was at my second conference in Las Vegas, there was a couple on the stage being recognized by the company president for having reached a top position. As they shared their story, the husband explained how, for the first four years, they didn't sell anything. His wife interrupted, "Honey, that's not quite true. We sold our house, our car, and our boat." But with time and perseverance, they reached the top.

I'm really busy building my business, talking to people, and helping my team. There's a meeting an hour away. Should I interrupt my cycle to go to the meeting?

Almost Right: You're kidding yourself that it's okay to miss an event.
Right: Getting all your people to every event within driving range.

Not everyone who goes to the meetings, or attends every event, makes $10,000 a month, but I can tell you that anybody making $10,000 a month is at every possible meeting and event. You may think that you don't need to be there, but your people need to be there, and you need to be there as an example. These events are a part of life in this business. If you've had a good day, the meeting needs you. If you've had a bad day, you need the meeting. The most important thing you can do as a leader is set the right example.

Sometimes people will say, "I'll go to the next event." The problem is that if they're not at the first event, they may not be around for the next event.

I'm building a team, but I find it to be a very frustrating process. What am I doing wrong?

Almost Right: Trying to manage your people.
Right: Focusing on setting the example by prospecting.

Management Mode

You go out and sponsor a few people, and now you want to manage them. The problem is that out of every ten people, only one or two will build their businesses. Maybe none of them will do anything. You just don't know until it happens.

Remember the 90/10 rule. Keep sponsoring. Keep out in front of the pack. Keep out-performing the rest of your people. You'll be setting the example—the right example. If you fall into a management role, your distributors will do the same. Soon everyone will be trying to manage the last new person who came in, trying to get that person to take action.

1. ??????
2. ?????????
3. ????????????????????

"There are three secrets of managing distributors. Unfortunately, no one knows what they are."
–Big Al

What do you do when you don't have a good sponsor?

> **Almost Right:** Try to do the business alone.
>
> **Right:** Go up line until you find someone in whom you have confidence.

I know exactly how you feel. I virtually never saw my sponsor after he rolled into town, enrolled me and I invested $5,000. He had no time for me. He got my $5,000, and had no interest in working with me. I had no idea what I was doing, but I sure couldn't afford to lose the money. I was very fortunate that I went to an event in Fargo, about seventy miles from home. I heard Mike Nelson, and I was blown away by his speech. As I said earlier, I went up to him after he spoke, and told him how my brother and I came to the conference to get re-motivated, and then we were going back to knocking on doors selling filters.

He was astounded. "I made over $200,000 last year and I never knocked on a door," he said. "Come up to my room later."

We did. We went up to his room and he explained the entire recruiting process. I learned two things that day—all about recruiting and the incredible value of going up line to find a mentor.

Don't be a victim or feel entitled

- ✓ It's not fair
- ✓ It shouldn't have
- ✓ Don't look for things to be perfect

"What happens, happens to us all. It's what we do about it that makes the difference." Jim Rohn

You will find this written on the gravestone of every distributor who failed: *"If only..."*

I've seen this many, many times. Something happens, and a distributor or a leader comes to me and tells me the whole story about how unfair it was. I understand and agree, but it happened and that's life. You can decide to dwell on it, and let it destroy your business, or you can accept that it happened and was not fair, and then move on.

Remember these three words: I am responsible.

Big But!

> Some of us have big, big buts. ....
> Understand that the word 'but' nullifies everything you said before it.
>
> I could do better 'but'.
>
> I'd like to go to that meeting 'but'.
>
> I'd like to get on the conference call 'but'.
>
> Taking responsibility means that we get rid of all those big 'buts'.

Some things have happened that are just not fair. I'm really discouraged.

Almost Right: Throw yourself a pity party.

Right: Accept the fact that life is not fair.

Bad things happen to good people. Don't be a victim. You will self-destruct your business. If you get all hung up on something that's not fair, you'll be angry your whole life. If something happened that shouldn't have happened, guess what? It still happened. Dwelling on it won't change it. If you dwell on something that shouldn't have happened, you'll spend your life feeling frustrated.

Don't look for things to be perfect. There's no company, no business, no product, and no person that is perfect. If you expect everything to be perfect, you'll be permanently disappointed.

Remember these three words every time you are faced with things that are not fair, are not perfect, or shouldn't have happened:

I am responsible.

So You Think You Have Problems

I'll never forget the day I was on stage at an event shaking hands with and being congratulated by the president and owner of the company. He said, "John, if there's anything I can do for you, let me know."

I said, "Well, if you could get the flies out of our fruit bars, it would go a long way."

Back then we had energy bars that tasted like cardboard. The problem was that when we opened them, all too often, we were confronted with fruit flies.

Try using one of those bars as a recruiting tool!

The Top of the Mountain looks so far.
It looks so far when you're just getting started and looking up.

When I got started in network marketing I thought, "If I could just earn $3,000 a month I would not know what to do with all that money."

Dream, visualize, imagine yourself at the top of your mountain and then take the first step. No matter how high the mountain the only way to get there is by taking one small step at a time.

> **_Think about it!_**
> **_It's the only way to the top._**

CHAPTER 13

I Feel Like Quitting

John, I sometimes get discouraged in this business. Did you ever reach a point when you wanted to quit and just chuck the whole thing?

Everyone has good days and bad days. I always tell people, "A bad day when following your dream is better than a good day at work." But still, everyone gets frustrated and entertains the idea of quitting. You're going to have down days; it comes with the territory. People who tell you that they've never felt like quitting are not being honest with themselves or with you. Of course, I've had days when I've felt like quitting. I've wondered if I have the strength, endurance, belief and patience to keep on keeping on.

When this happens, I do a couple of things. First, I look at the alternatives:

- ✓ In the real world, I'm worth about $10 an hour.

- ✓ I would have to be at work by 8:00 every morning, and many evenings I would still be working at 7:00 or 8:00, or later.

- ✓ I would be on call twenty-four hours a day, seven days a week.

- ✓ I would see much less of my family.

With this in mind, look at your alternatives:

- ✓ Would you want to go back to your prior occupation?

- ✓ If you're doing your business part-time, do you want to be totally dependent on your current job for the rest of your life?

- ✓ Do you want your destiny to be in the hands of someone else who can tell you goodbye at the drop of a hat?

The next thing I do is get back to my motivational CD's. The cure for "stinkin thinkin" is to input the good stuff. If you keep thinking about the good stuff, your whole attitude will change.

> *A bad day when following your dream*
> *is better than a good day at work.*

One of the biggest challenges you'll face in building your own business is yourself. The challenge is working on yourself to stay positive, focused, motivated and disciplined. Ultimately your success is up to you. Success is an inside job.

Another thing you can do is review your goals, and remind yourself of your "why." This by itself can be a very motivating exercise. Remind yourself that if you're not going to follow through, if you quit, then you'll have to give up all your goals:

- ✓ I'm not going to have a new house.
- ✓ I'm not going to get the new car I want.
- ✓ I'm not going to have a retirement fund.
- ✓ The kids won't be able to go to college.

Keep your "why" in front of you. It will keep you focused and keep you going. When you feel like quitting, look at your alternatives, refocus on your "why," review your goals, and get moving.

This is how you'll separate yourself from the pack, from the mass of people who lead lives of quiet desperation. If you feel like quitting, you're normal. Just don't quit.

> *There is no courage without fear.*

> *You miss 100 percent of the shots you don't take.*
> *–Wayne Gretsky*

> *The speed of the leader sets the speed of the pack.*

CHAPTER 14

NINETY DAYS TO CHANGE YOUR LIFE

To change your life, the first step is a 90-day commitment that you'll do whatever it takes for the next 90 days to get your business off the ground. Get up an hour earlier or stay up an hour later—whatever you need to do. Network marketing is like a big flywheel. You have to keep cranking on it to get it spinning, but once it is spinning, all you have to do is tap it occasionally to keep it going.

Imagine an airplane taxiing down the runway. The plane will lift off at 100 miles per hour. What happens if it goes only 90 miles an hour? Nothing happens! It doesn't get off the ground. It could taxi from here to Fargo, and it wouldn't get off the ground. Once it takes off, however, much less energy is needed to keep the plane in the air than was needed to get it off the ground.

The same is true with network marketing. Your runway is 90 days. Do whatever it takes to attain liftoff, to get off the ground. Put the throttle to the wall. You want to build your business in 90-day windows. If you've been involved for six months, a year, or maybe longer, you can turn around and take another approach. You can tell your prospects that you've been involved for as long as you have, but that you didn't know what you were doing, and that you weren't doing things right. Then tell them what happened in the last 90 days.

Once you achieve liftoff, you can back off a little on the throttle because you have other people supporting you, building their organizations and yours. Your business will take less energy to maintain than it took to get started.

A fast start is always, always, always the best start.

Over the last twenty-five years, I've earned $14 million. I often say that I really earned that $14 million in my first 90 days. If you do the 90-day blitz to get your business off the ground, it sets the wheels in motion to pay you for a lifetime.

People don't quit network marketing because they're not making enough money,
but because they're losing money.

The Inside Step:

Whatever step is going on in your mind you are attracting into your life.

Your mind is an incredible tool.

It is more powerful than the most powerful computer in the world and it's yours, all yours, to use as you see fit.

Napoleon Hill said "Whatever the mind can conceive and believe it can achieve."

✓ How do you direct your thoughts?

✓ What do you think about most of the time?

CHAPTER 15

PERSONAL GROWTH

John, one of the things that you talk about all the time is personal development. You say that what you become in this business is far more important than the money you make.

> **Almost Right:** Know that the material is important and review it once.
> **Right:** Know that the material is important and review it many, many times.

There is no question in my mind that personal growth is the key to success in network marketing. As Jim Rohn, perhaps North America's leading business philosopher, says, "Work harder on yourself than you do at your job. When you work at your job, you make a living. When you work on yourself, you'll make a fortune."

Network marketing is pretty simple. A big part of the business is that people buy people. You need to become buyable. I believe that my commitment to ongoing personal growth is responsible for 80 percent of the success I've enjoyed. Obviously, you must have the commitment and the burning desire to follow your personal growth with action—with doing the right things to build your business.

People ask me, "John, what are the things that make the most difference?"

My first response is always, "Personal growth," meaning a commitment to become more, so that you can do more and have more. I often quote from some of my favorite audio programs. Napoleon Hill, in his book, *Think and Grow Rich*, emphasizes fundamentals that don't change regardless of the business or profession. Hill, and other similar speakers and writers, talk a lot about fundamentals, principles and philosophies. They also talk about reshaping your life, one step at a time, by changing your philosophies.

> *Make a commitment to BE more,*
> *so that you can DO more and HAVE more.*
>
> –Zig Ziglar

Jim Rohn talks about being twenty-five, behind on his rent, behind on his payments, behind on his promises, and broke. His mentor asked, "Why are you continuing to do what's not working? Who sold you on that philosophy?" I was amazed by this. How true!

A few years back, I purchased a Tony Robbins tape set. When I started listening to the second tape, Tony said, "Congratulations. You've done what 97 out of 100 people who buy this tape set never do—get to tape two." Wow, imagine spending $179 for a tape set and then not listening to it.

Could you give us an example of personal development in your life?

The best example is my journey from one extreme to another. What better illustration of personal growth is there than my journey from school (struggling with dyslexia, trying to be invisible, and being afraid of my own shadow), to going to work as a maintenance manager, then to going into networking marketing and being treated as an equal, to ultimately receiving a standing ovation from 8,000 professionals in Orlando? Tell me that personal growth isn't important! Tell me that you don't grow as a person in this business!

In network marketing, the first thing that blew me away was being treated as an equal by successful individuals who were making more in a month than I was making in a year. This was so much different from how I'd been treated in the company environment to which I was accustomed.

What if my business grows and I don't?

If your business grows and you don't, it's very unlikely that you'll be able to hold on to your success. There are people all through this industry who were lucky. They got started with the right company at the right time, enrolled a few good people, and rode their business to a level of success way beyond themselves. Then they lost it all. They have continued to chase that experience from company to company with no success, never being able to recapture their former glory.

Why? This happened because their business grew, but they didn't. They made the mistake of thinking that they knew it all, and that it was all them. They began to believe their own press releases.

To have and sustain success in this business, you absolutely must invest in personal development. I believe to the core of my being that the consistent level of success I've enjoyed over the last 25 years, having earned over $14 million and helping my teams earn over $250 million, would not have happened without my commitment to personal growth.

There are a lot of great books, audios and information on personal development. It can be a bit overwhelming to wade through it all, so let me get you started. The person who has had the greatest impact and influence on me, who has led me to the fortune I've achieved, is Jim Rohn. His four-CD set "Challenge to Succeed" is an absolute must-have. You can find this series and many others at www.rightoralmostright.com.

You might be thinking that if 80 percent of my success came from my commitment to personal development— listening to and reading the books—then that was pretty easy to do. But it's also pretty easy not to do. You can think of this as one of the small steps I talked about earlier. The decision to do or not to do can have an enormous influence on the outcome of your life.

There Is Always A Cost.

What will it cost to pursue your dream?

The cost of pursuing your dream is infinitely less than the cost of letting your dream die.

The cost of neglect is far, far greater than the cost of discipline.

CHAPTER 16

REWARDS OF THE JOURNEY

Vacations ... Freedom ... Missions ... Dream Homes

*You say, "It's easy to have a great attitude,
just look at her success." I say this,
"Maybe the success is there because of her attitude."*

–Jim Rohn on attitude

John, sometimes I just want to go back to some nice, safe 9-to-5 job with a regular pay check every week. Tell me again what happens if I keep on keeping on.

What happens when you focus on your dream—when you move through the rejections, the sacrifices and the early years of just getting by? What happens when you overcome the negative self-talk, slip quietly around the dream-stealers, and keep on keeping on? You arrive at the lifestyle you imagined for yourself.

In fact, network marketing can change your life in ways that are beyond your imagination. What have you envisioned for yourself? All of these things are possible for you. If others have done it, why can't you do it? If I did it, why can't you do it?

Rewards of the Journey

The network marketing journey has so many rewards that affect every aspect of life.

Personal Freedom

You can attain personal freedom with no company to work for, no boss to answer to, no customers to jump for and no clients to please.

> *Is there any other profession in the entire world where you can put your family first?*

Family

You can put your family first and work your schedule around your family so that you're able to attend every event. When other parents are putting in overtime, you're there at the Little League baseball game cheering on your kids. Do you think they will remember this? Of course they will. Instead of being stuck at the office, you can be there when your family needs you. When your son or daughter has the flu, you're there to bring them chicken soup.

Travel

There comes a point in network marketing when the world becomes your playground. You can travel to any place at any time, and not be concerned about the money or the time you're taking from your business. When you get home, there will be no emergencies to deal with, and no panicked calls about issues that only you can fix. There may, however, be a larger paycheck than the one you received the month before you took off.

Recognition

One of every individual's deepest needs is the hunger for recognition, to be acknowledged for their contributions. There is no place like network marketing for recognition. When you think of recognition, you often visualize the public on-stage events that celebrate major milestones on your journey. Recognition comes from many other sources in network marketing. The most meaningful recognition is to see one of your distributors using your advice and training to accomplish his or her goals. When one of your distributors sees his or her dream becoming reality, the satisfaction cannot compete with any form of public recognition. There is also a quiet personal satisfaction as you move through major milestones.

Financial Freedom

You can have money in the bank, and every debt paid in full. You can have investments, a house that is mortgage free, and cars that are 100 percent yours.

Time When You Need It

Does it get more important than this? When my youngest daughter was just four years old she suffered second- and third-degree burns to her face, shoulder and chest. As you can imagine, she was in great pain and we had to change her bandages several times a day. I lay in bed with her for an entire month watching Barney. It created a very strong bond between us. I'm sure I can recite every Barney song ever written. I now think, *"What an incredible business I have. If I'd had a regular job, I might have been able to take off a day or two. After that, my employer might have felt badly, but he would've been telling me that it was time to get back to work."*

But I was in network marketing. I got overwhelming support from the company and my distributors. I didn't have to ask permission for time off. I was able to take the time that I thought she needed. And my business still grew.

Circle of Friends

Would you like to have a circle of friends who are relentlessly upbeat, always positive, always focused on growing and helping others to grow? This is the kind of people you'll be with, and grow with, in a network marketing company.

My Own Example

Here's another one of my does-it-get-any-better-than-this examples. I have a lake house in Minnesota, and during the winter I live in Florida. I'm able to spend a large part of every day with my family. I have friends in fifty states and four countries. With one phone call, I can be picked up at any major airport in the country, and treated like a visiting celebrity.

My income is in the top 1/10 of 1 percent of the top earners in North America. Money is no longer a major consideration in my life. The news that one of my leaders has qualified for their next pin level means more to me than my next paycheck.

Most meaningful for me is the personal freedom I have to do what I want to do, with whom I want to do it, when I want to do it, and where I want to do it. I associate with people I enjoy being with from both a business and a social perspective.

One of the most significant rewards of network marketing is the quality of life that it has made possible for me, particularly the amount of time I can spend with my family and children. Once, as I was leaving on one of my trips, my younger daughter, Nicole, asked, "Dad, do you have to go?"

My oldest daughter, Stephanie, pointed out, "Nicole, we get to see our dad way more than anyone else gets to see their dad."

Extraordinary Experiences of Success

The extraordinary experiences of success in network marketing go well beyond the personal and financial freedom, recognition and relationships. These are experiences that most people never imagine or dream of. These experiences are typically those that you see only celebrities enjoying.

Thus far, I have:

- ✓ sailed with Winston Cuppers;

- ✓ played baseball with Hall of Famers;

- ✓ attended mystery dinners with celebrities such as Peter Fonda and Peter Graves;

- ✓ attended private concerts with some of the best well-known artists;

- ✓ eaten dinner with Roger Staubach, hosted by Wolfgang Puck;

- ✓ gone on all-expense-paid vacations at some of the world's most exclusive resorts.

These are experiences that I could have never, ever imagined back when I was maintenance manager at the Barrel of Fun potato chip plant. But through network marketing, they've become my reality.

> *Network marketing is not a job; it is a lifestyle.*
> *Network marketing is simply a better way to live*

No Results Yet?

The results will come.

Focus on doing the right things everyday, everyday, everyday.

Evaluate yourself based on your activity, not your results.

What did I DO today?

If you aren't doing, you're dying. Life is doing.

Keep on doing.

Keep on taking those Small Steps to the TOP.

CHAPTER 17

WHERE DO YOU GO FROM HERE?

Now that we've talked about my journey, I'm sure you'd like to talk about yours—about how you can reap the benefits of network marketing. Just where do you go from here?

Here are the steps that will take you to the top:

- ✓ Remember the Small Step philosophy: "Every decision you make counts."

- ✓ Remember that people buy people. It's your passion, posture, beliefs and enthusiasm that influence others to join or follow you.

- ✓ Remember your mind-set. If your thinking is stinking, your business is shrinking.

- ✓ Be consistent. This is an everyday business; whether it's an hour a day or ten hours a day. It's every day, every day, every day. If you're not consistent in your efforts, you'll be starting over all the time.

- ✓ Be committed. No one will follow you if you don't demonstrate and exemplify an all-in commitment. For example, everything you do sets an example of what others think they have to do. They will copy your good habits as well as your bad habits.

- ✓ Know your goals and your "WHY." Put your goals and your "WHY" in writing, and review them twice a day.

- ✓ Invest in your personal development. This is a simple step that's easy to do, but it's also easy *not* to do it.

- ✓ Implement your DMO (daily method of operation). Plan your day on paper before it starts. Prioritize, and remember that you get paid for talking to people who are not doing your business or using your products.

Implement a personal check-up. Ask yourself these questions, especially in areas where you struggle:

✓ How am I doing?

✓ How can I do better?

✓ Take responsibility. When things happen that are not fair, not perfect, or uncalled for—and believe me, they will. Remember these three words: I am responsible.

> *I am responsible.*

PERSONAL DEVELOPMENT IS CRITICAL

When I think about personal development, I'm reminded of an old fable about Mount Olympus. Many years ago in ancient Greece, a traveler met an old man on the road and asked him how to get to Mount Olympus. The old man, who happened to be Socrates, replied by saying, "If you really want to get to Mount Olympus, just make sure that every step you take is in that direction."

The moral of the fable is simple. If you want to be successful, if you want to see your dream become your reality, be sure that every step you take is in that direction.

> *Work harder on yourself than you work on your job. When you work on your job, you can make a living; when you work on yourself, you can make a fortune.*
>
> **–Jim Rohn**

The following tape sets (now CD's, mp3 or digital product) are the personal development tools that have been most valuable for me:

Zig Ziglar

"Goal Setting Program"
"Developing the Qualities of Success"

Jim Rohn

"Building Your Network Marketing Business"

(This CD is a must-listen to many, many times over.)

"The Art of Exceptional Living"

"Challenge to Succeed in the 90's"

"Making of a Leader for the 90's, Volume 1"

"Making of a Leader for the 90's, Volume 2"

"The Power of Ambition"

"Take Charge of Your Life"

Earl Nightingale

"Lead the Field"

"The Strangest Secret"

"Communicating What You Think"

Dale Carnegie

"How to Win Friends and Influence People"

SOME FINAL WORDS

Thank you for buying and reading my book. I wish you the very best in this amazing industry.

I recently spent 6 days on an incredible 2,300-mile motorcycle ride through some of the most beautiful country in the United States. We rode through the Black Hills of South Dakota, the Big Horn and Bear Tooth Mountains in Wyoming and Montana, and on to Yellowstone Park. As I was riding, I had a lot of time to think and reflect on my life, and how I got to where I am. I asked myself, "How did this happen?" Three words came to mind: consistency, faith, and focus.

Consistency: I've been doing the business every day, every day, every day, doing what I had to do even when I didn't feel like doing it. I've kept repeating my story to anyone and everyone who would listen.

Faith: In spite of my challenges, setbacks, obstacles and naysayers, I had faith that my business would work. There were difficult days when success seemed impossible, but I kept the faith. I kept on keeping on.

Focus: I refused to get distracted by life, by others or by the next "sure thing" hot deal that came by. I stayed focused on what I was doing.

These three words—consistency, faith, and focus—led me to my fortune, and they can take you to your dream life in network marketing, too.

You can say it was wisdom or just good luck. All I know is that I'm in the right industry, at the right time, and I believe network marketing can work for you as well.

I will see you at the top!

With my very best wishes,

John

ABOUT THE AUTHOR

John Haremza is a network-marketing veteran with 25 years in the business and earnings in excess of $14 million. He has averaged over $1 million a year for the last 10 years. But his all-time proudest accomplishment has been leading his people to earnings of over $250 million and changing countless lives.

John's story is a true American rags-to-riches tale, with his journey going from the humblest of beginnings in Perham, Minnesota, to a world-class network marketing leader. His message is simple: "If I can do it with my challenges and background, then you can do it." He is living proof that you can be successful in this business regardless of your education, background or finances.

John has an uncanny ability to communicate the fundamentals, philosophies and principles of success so that they're easy to understand and implement. He has been referred to by many of his peers as the "Jim Rohn of network marketing."

Prior to being introduced to network marketing, John worked as a maintenance manager in a small potato chip factory. He had never sold anything in his life, and had no business experience. He also had dyslexia, a severe learning disability. Back then, he had one objective—to be invisible. He felt fortunate to get a high school diploma.

Now, John has been featured in multiple publications, such as Stephen Covey's *7 Habits of Highly Effective Networkers, Network Marketing Times* and *Your Business at Home Magazine* (on the cover). He has also been named one of the top twenty-one marketing leaders in the world in John Milton Fogg's recent book, *The Greatest Networkers in the World.*

John's leadership has transformed countless lives. He has friends and business associates around the world, and his wisdom will help you to make your dream a reality. Network marketing is an amazing industry with wonderful products, and incredible opportunities. As John says, "Network marketing changed my life in ways that were far beyond my imagination."

> **You will see me at the top of the mountain or dead along the side, but never at the bottom.**